DEVON *and* CORNWALL

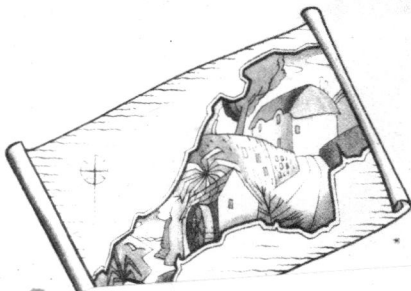

W. & R. Chambers *Ltd.,*
LONDON & EDINBURGH

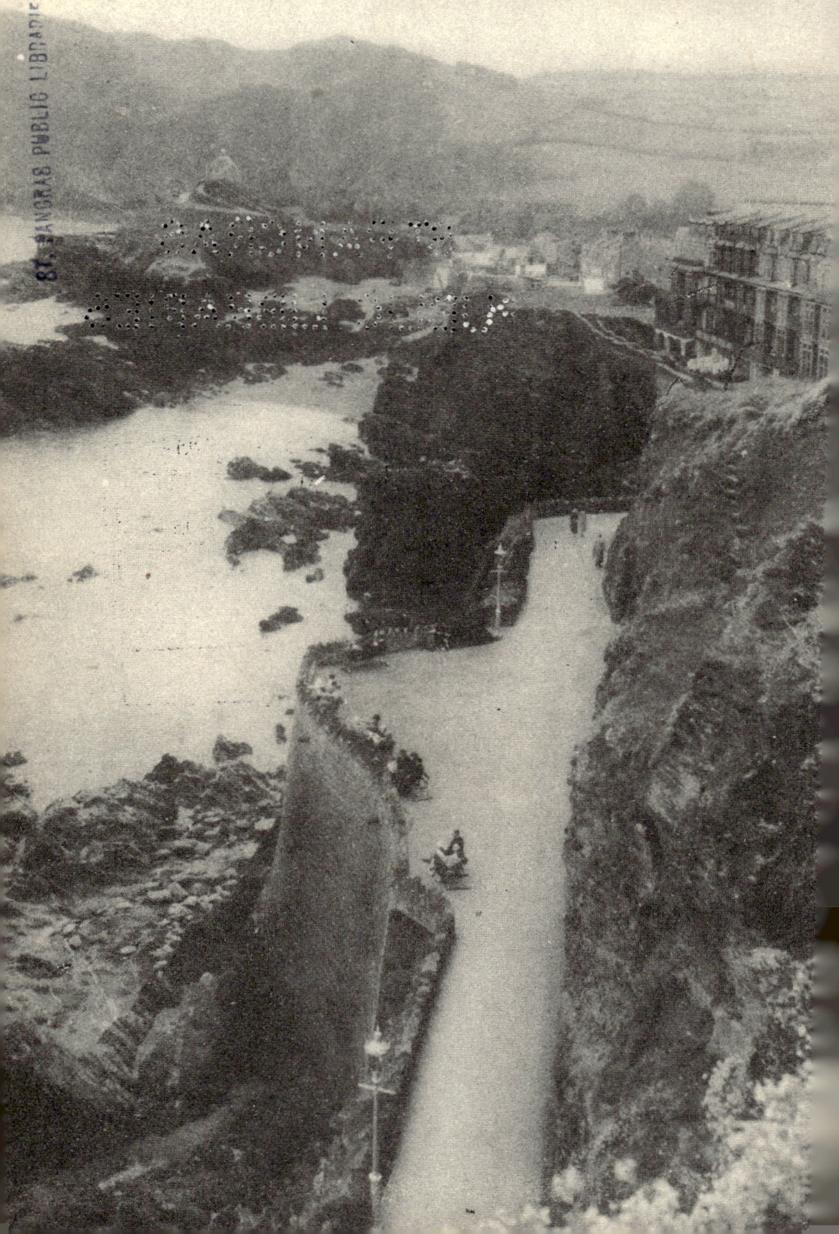

Printed in Great Britain by Horrocks & Co. Ltd., Ashton-under-Lyne

Facing : The Coast at Ilfracombe.

Estuary of the Torridge at Appledore

APPLEDORE ('apple-tree'). A town and seaport on the Torridge estuary, 7 miles WSW. of Barnstaple. Local industries include the collection of mussels, cockles and 'laver,' a species of edible seaweed.

Appledore has yachting, sea-fishing and bathing facilities.

At 'Bloody Corner' near-by is a burial-stone to Hubba the Dane, routed here by the locals in the reign of King Alfred.

A tablet commemorates this as follows:

'Stop, Stranger, Stop. Near this spot lies buried King Hubba the Dane who was slain by King Alfred the Great in a bloody retreat.'

ASHBURTON (ash'burton). A town on the Yeo, *c.* 19 miles SW. of Exeter, with a fine Gothic church.

A house in North Street has slates cut to represent the four card suits, and an ancient grammar school building was founded in 1314.

There is good trout fishing in the neighbourhood.

AXMINSTER. A market town on the Axe, *c.* 25 miles ENE. of Exeter, traditionally one of the sites of the great battle of Brunanburgh (937) between Athelstan and the Danes.

The church has a Norman door and Jacobean pulpit, and near it is part of the old factory (1755) of the former Axminster carpet industry, which ceased in 1835. South of Axminster are the remains of Newnham Abbey.

There is trout fishing in the Axe.

AXMOUTH, near the mouth of the Axe, *c.* 21 miles E. of Exeter, has an ancient camp on Hawksdown Hill above it, and good mediæval wall paintings in its church.

There is an 18-hole golf course here.

BAMPTON. A market town surrounded by hills, *c.* 20 miles N. of Exeter, notable for an annual fair (Oct.) of Exmoor ponies, cattle and sheep.

Its church has some sixteenth-century stained glass.

There is trout fishing in the Exe close by.

8

BARNSTAPLE

A BOROUGH, claimed to be the oldest in the kingdom, and river port on the Taw near its estuary, crossed here by a fine, ancient bridge of sixteen arches.

The mound upon which an eleventh-century castle stood may still be seen. Ships to meet the Spanish Armada were equipped here; the townsfolk sided with Parliament on the outbreak of the Civil Wars, and the town changed hands four times in the struggle. It welcomed as settlers many fugitive Huguenots on the Revocation of the Edict of Nantes.

Outstanding buildings are the Guildhall, containing forty portraits by Hudson and Reynolds, and the municipal insignia (two maces, a mayor's chain and badge, and a silver oar), the churches of St. Peter (chiefly fourteenth-century) with its twisted lead spire, St. Mary the Virgin (thirteenth-century) and Penrose's Almshouses.

Taw Vale Parade and Queen Anne's Walk are pleasant riverside ways. There is trout fishing in the Taw and its tributaries.

BIDEFORD (bid'i-ford). An ancient borough and market town on the Torridge, here spanned by a twenty-four arched, fifteenth-century bridge, 8 miles SW. of Barnstaple.

It has fine old houses, notably that which now forms part of the Royal Hotel (see the ceiling of the Oak Room). Spanish cannon, old relics of the Armada, can be seen in the park. There are tennis courts and good bowling greens, and a famous golf course at Westward Ho! (see article).

There is trout fishing in the Torridge and its affluents and in the Cor-

The old Grammar School at Barnstaple.

From an old Engraving of Brixham and Torbay.

poration reservoirs. Rowing and sailing are also available on the river.

BRIXHAM.
A picturesque town and fishing port, with steep side streets and fascinating harbour, *c.* 6 miles S. of Torquay.

A statue with inscriptions in English and Dutch commemorates the landing here of William of Orange in 1688. The composer of 'Abide With Me,' the Rev. H. F. Lyte, was vicar of All Saints Church, which has a carillon of some of his hymns.

There is a cavern here in which finds have included the bones of the cave lion, hyena and rhinoceros. Brixham's fishing fleet was once famous.

Brixham has tennis courts, bowling greens, and an open-air bathing pool.

BUCKFASTLEIGH.
A small town of narrow streets, on the Dart, *c.* 15 miles W. of Torquay, with Buckfast Abbey to the N. Of this originally Norman abbey the Abbot's tower dates from the fifteenth century, but the remainder has been built by monks of the Benedictine order since 1882. It was consecrated in 1932 and completed in 1937. Buckfastleigh has an interesting old church.

There are bowling greens here. Salmon and trout fishing is to be had in the Dart.

BUDLEIGH SALTERTON
(named from old monastic salt-works here). A small seaport and residential place on the south coast at the mouth of the Otter, *c.* 12 miles SE. of Exeter. It has good bathing, a sports ground, tennis courts, bowling greens and an 18-hole golf course (East Devon Golf Club).

CHAGFORD.
A quiet little market town, *c.* 14 miles WSW. of Exeter, contains the interesting Three Crowns Hotel, with its stone mullions, former private residence of the Whyddons. Whyddon Park, anciently a seat of the family, is worth visiting.

Numerous ancient crosses are to be found near Chagford.

Good salmon and trout fishing is available in the Teign here. There is a small cinema, swimming pool and bowling green.

CHUDLEIGH. A picturesque small town on the side of a hill, *c.* 8 miles SW. of Exeter. Within easy reach of sea and moors, this is an excellent tourist centre. Chudleigh Reeks and the Pixie's Cave attract many visitors. In this cliff cavern numerous prehistoric relics have been unearthed.

The much-restored chancel screen of the church has paintings of apostles and prophets in its panels. Ugbrooke House, a mile away, seat of the Clifford family, has an extensive park containing 'Dryden's Grove' (said to have been frequented by the poet).

Chudleigh has tennis courts and bowling greens, and there is trout fishing in the Teign near-by.

Buckfast Abbey—Right: Interior.
Below: Exterior.

CLOVELLY

A FASCINATING place on a precipitous site on Bideford Bay, *c.* 20 miles WSW. of Barnstaple. This is a very popular summer resort, not least because of its excellent walking and boating facilities.

Its cobbled main street, flanked by picturesque houses, descends to a little stone harbour. The church, an ancient building, contains interesting monuments to the Cary family, a mediæval hour-glass, and a Saxon font.

Towards Bideford is the beautiful "Hobby" wood walk. Clovelly Dykes, an early Iron-Age encampment, lies 1 mile to the south. Through the grounds of Clovelly Court, a Georgian house built in 1789, a path leads to the famous Gallantry Bower (387 feet), an almost sheer cliff.

Clovelly should be seen in the evening from a small boat in the bay.

COLYTON. A town in the Coly valley near the south coast, *c.* 22 miles E. of Exeter.

The Great House here was the former residence of the family of Yonge. Colcombe Castle, to the north, mostly ruinous, was built by Hugh de Courtenay, Earl of Devon, at the end of the thirteenth century. Part of its buildings now constitute a farm house. Colyton has a fine church with traces of Saxon masonry, and a lace-making industry is still carried on.

Colyford, to the south, was anciently a borough.

CREDITON. Named from

Clovelly—Above: Looking down towards the Harbour. Facing: The main Street.

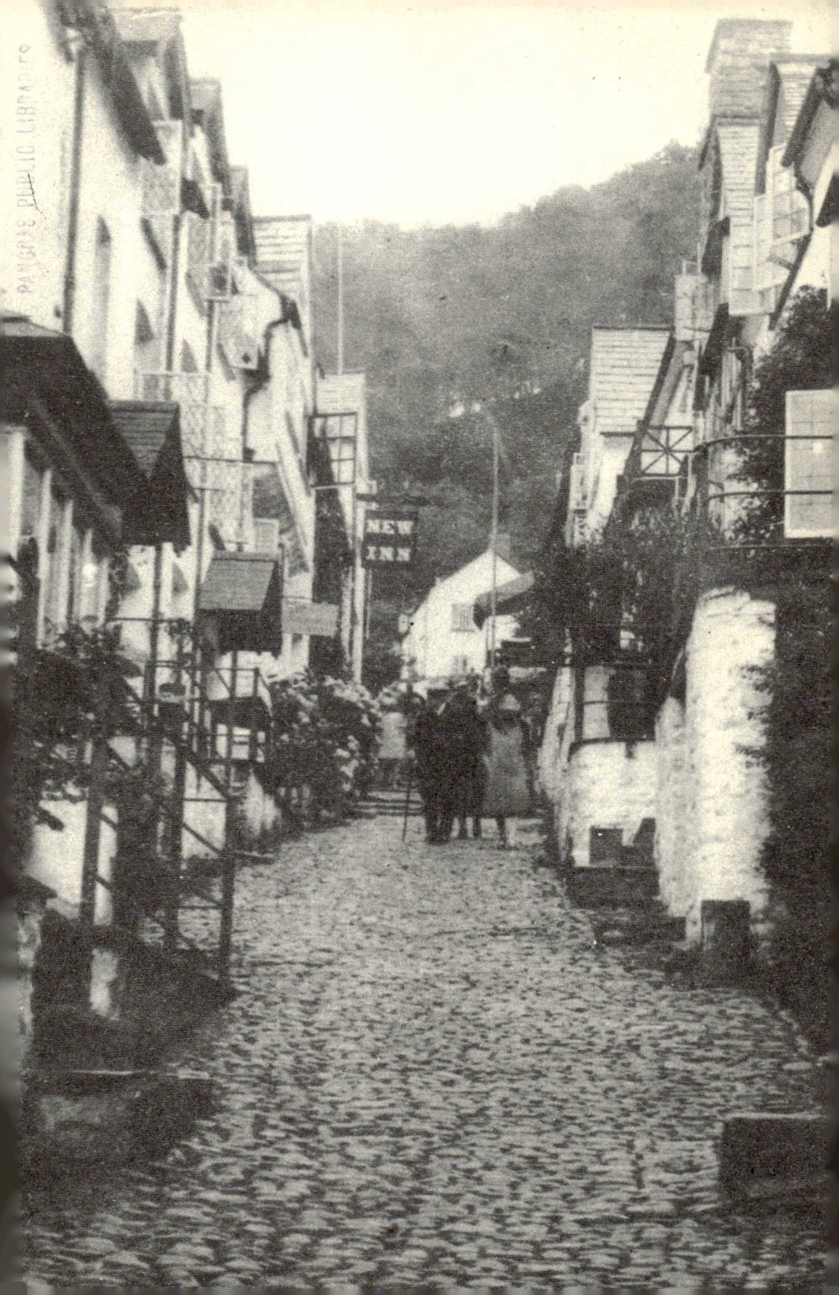
NEW
INN

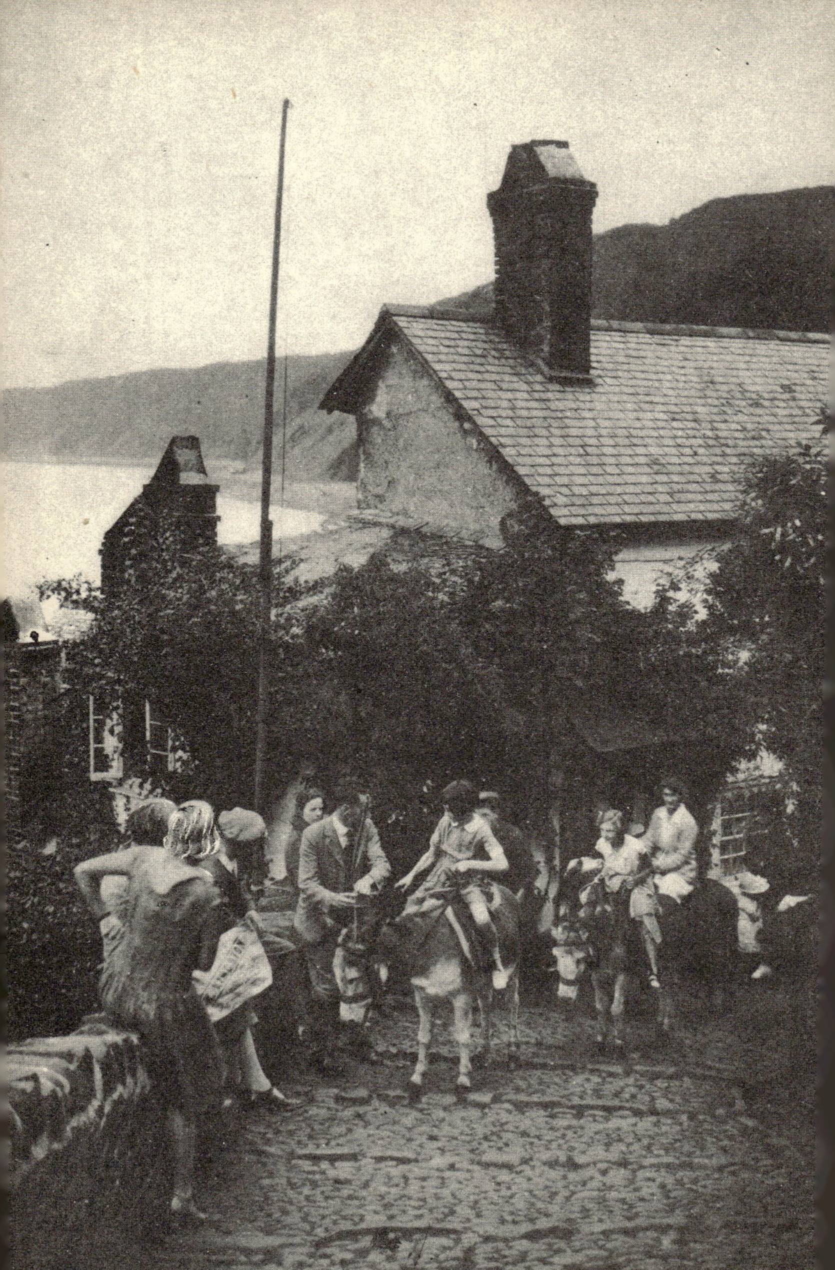

the Creedy, on which it stands, *c.* 7 miles NW. of Exeter, anciently a city and bishop's see, Crediton has a strikingly beautiful red sandstone Perpendicular church and Lady Chapel.

There is a 9-hole golf course, hunting with the Silverton Foxhounds, and local trout fishing. Good cider, sweets, medicinal lozenges and dried milk are manufactured here, and there was formerly a notable woollen and boot industry. It is the town which serves perhaps the richest agricultural land in Devon. The principal market of the year is April Great Market, on the third Saturday in April. A pleasure fair is held in August. The Boys' Grammar School has an Elizabethan charter.

CULLOMPTON (cul'lompton). A town on the Culm with streams in its main street, *c.* 13 miles NE. of Exeter.

Its ancient church has a fine tower, a coloured roof, and notable fan tracery and carving in the Lane Aisle or Chapel.

The Walronds, an Elizabethan mansion, was used as a convent and is now a private residence. The arms of the Petre family are on the oak mantelpiece in the dining-hall. Hillersdon House, a large mansion, is near Cullompton.

There is good trout fishing in the Culm here.

♫ALUTING *the* APPLE TREE

Custom was to place cakes on the branches and pour cider on the roots—traceable to the pre-Christian sacrifices to the fruit-tree goddess—declaiming this rhyme:
Here's to thee, Old Apple Tree,
Whence thou may'st bud, and whence thou may'st blow,
And whence thou may'st bear apples, enow!
Hats full! Caps full!
Bushel by bushel— sacks full,
And my pockets full too! Hurra!

Facing: Donkeys at Clovelly.
Right: An old Devon Manor.

15

EXETER

The Great Cathedral Town of the South-West

EXETER is the county town of Devon, a municipal borough and seat of a bishop, on a hill overlooking the Exe. It has a large number of excellent hotels, cafés, and shops, five good cinemas, swimming baths, tennis courts, bowling greens and an 18-hole golf course. There is trout fishing to be had in the neighbourhood. Train and bus services to all the surrounding towns and villages make Exeter one of the best holiday haunts in the south- west country.

The Cathedral. *Exterior.*—The Norman transept towers are the only parts that remain of the early twelfth-century building begun by Bishop Warlewast. The Lady Chapel is thirteenth-century, and the great part of the remainder is fourteenth-century in the Decorated style. The west front has sixty-eight statues, including those of Athelstan and Edward the Confessor on either side of the west window. The other figures represent mostly kings of England and biblical characters, among them Noah, Gideon, Samson and Samuel.

Interior.—The richly vaulted nave contains on the north wall the Minstrel's Gallery with sculptured angels playing musical instruments. In the north transept is a thirteenth-century astronomical clock. The north tower houses the Great Peter bell. The south transept includes a monument to the second Earl of Devon, Hugh de Courtenay, and his wife. From this transept access is gained to

Above: Exeter Cathedral (West Front)   Facing: Exeter Guildhall.

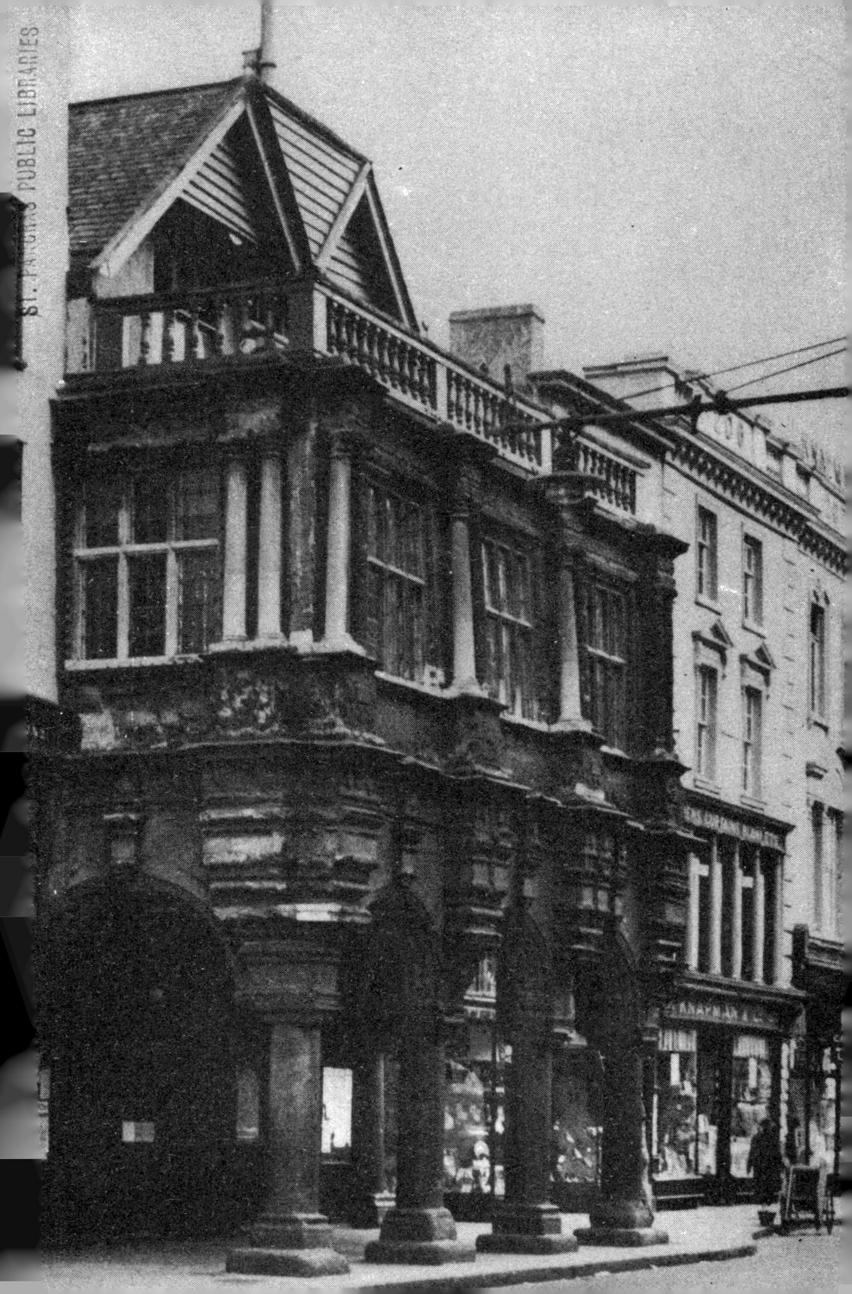
ST. PANCRAS PUBLIC LIBRARIES

Entrance Arch of Rougemont Castle, Exeter.

the Chapter House, former home of the valuable Cathedral library. The choir (thirteenth-century) shows early Norman masonry, a fourteenth-century screen with fifteenth-century paintings and fascinating misereres, of mermen, mermaids, elephants and all manner of creatures, in the stalls. The Bishop's Throne dates from the fifteenth century. There is a modern alabaster reredos. The east window has perpendicular tracery and ancient glass. The Lady Chapel has interesting monuments, a good roof and reredos (partly ancient).

The Cathedral was much damaged by air bombardment during the Second World War (1939-45).

The Palace Gardens and Bishop's Palace (1387) lie adjacent to the Cathedral.

Interesting Churches in Exeter

Saxon or Norman features are to be found in the churches of St. Pancras (Norman font), St. Petroch's (Saxon and Norman masonry), St. Stephen's (Saxon crypt), while the fascinating St. Mary Steps has a curious old clock and fine painted rood screen. Enemy bombardment during the Second World War destroyed St. Mary Arches (Norman arcades), St. Lawrence, and St. Sidwell's (with its carvings of St. Sidwell, Exeter's saint).

Moll's Coffee House.

Other Ancient Buildings

The Guildhall (1330), with its striking entrance, one of the oldest municipal buildings in Britain, contains a fine hall with vaulted ceiling and old panelling, as well as many valuable portraits.

Tuckers Hall (1471), the Elizabethan Moll's Coffee House (now Worth's), with an elegant oak-panelled room, Bampfylde House, and Rougemont Castle and grounds should certainly be visited, and the circuit of Exeter city walls may still be traced easily. Quaint old houses are very numerous.

Museums, Galleries, Cultural Buildings

The Royal Albert Memorial Museum and Art Gallery contains excellent natural history and archæological collections, as well as valuable modern pictures, and there is a good city library. Exeter is the seat of University College of the South-west of England.

The "Blind Days"

In former times the first three days of March were considered by Devon farmers to be the unlucky 'blind days,' and upon them no farmer would sow any seed.

These days, often stormy, have been by some identified with the similarly ill-omened 'borrowed days' from April.

Thatched Roofs at Denbury Village.

EXMOUTH. A much-favoured holiday resort on the south coast, at the mouth of the Exe, *c.* 10 miles SE. of Exeter.

Fishing is the chief local industry. There is an 18-hole golf course, tennis courts and bowling green.

Cure for AGUES

"It is usual with many persons in Exeter, who are affected with agues, to visit at dead of night the nearest cross-road five different times and there bury a new-laid egg. The visit is paid about an hour before the cold fit is expected; and they are persuaded that with the egg they shall bury the ague.

If the experiment fail, they attribute it to some unlucky accident that may have befallen them on the way."

Douce's MS. Notes.

HARTLAND, or HARTON. A small town near the bold Hartland Point (with a lighthouse and fog-horn), on the north coast, *c.* 22 miles WSW. of Barnstaple. It has the distinction of being the farthest from railways in England.

The stately church of St. Nectan has a fine western tower (128 feet, said to be the highest in Devon) and an ancient rood screen.

Hartland Abbey was anciently a college of regular canons, but of it there are few remains except the name. Near-by are Hartland Quay and Speke's Mill Mouth, with a 70-foot waterfall, both of which are interesting.

HATHERLEIGH. A small town, *c.* 19 miles S. of Barnstaple.

There is a holy well, formerly noted for healing properties, and another, a baptismal well, on the moor close by.

Good trout fishing is to be had in the Lew, Torridge and other streams here, and there are bowling greens.

HONITON. A picturesque borough, with good hotels, cafés and shops, *c.* 17 miles ENE. of Exeter, gives name to a species of fine lace made here and elsewhere in the southwest. There is a local handmade pottery industry.

St. Michael's church, on the slope to the S. of Honiton, has vestiges of a fine old carved screen and the tomb of Marwood, Queen Elizabeth's physician. St. Margaret's Almshouses on the Exeter road were originally a fourteenth-century leper hospital. There is a tower (80 feet) erected by Coplestone, Bishop of Llandaff, on Honiton Hill to the south-east, and a prehistoric camp on Dumpdon Hill to the north.

Honiton has a 9-hole golf course.

Some Devonshire Golf Courses

	Day	Week
AXE CLIFF (Seaton)	3/-	12/6
BIGBURY	5/-	25/-
CHURSTON	5/-	21/-
CREDITON	2/6	10/-
EAST DEVON (Budleigh Salterton)	5/-	25/-
EXETER	4/-	15/-
EXMOUTH	4/-	20/-
HONITON	2/6	12/6
ILFRACOMBE	5/-	20/-
MANOR HOUSE (North Bovey)	5/-	20/-
MANOR HOUSE (Moretonhampstead)	5/-	
OKEHAMPTON	5/-	30/-
ROYAL NORTH DEVON (Westward Ho!)	5/-	25/-
SIDMOUTH	3/6	17/6
TAVISTOCK	5/-	20/-
TEIGNMOUTH	3/6	15/-
THURLESTONE	7/-	25/-
TIVERTON	3/6	20/-
TORBAY (Paignton)	5/-	25/-
TORQUAY	5/-	21/-
YELVERTON	5/-	15/-

The sea-front at Ilfracombe: Capstone Hill and the Pier.

ILFRACOMBE

A SEASIDE town, favourite summer and winter resort, and unsurpassed walking centre, on the north coast, *c.* 11 miles NNE. of Barnstaple.

Above its natural and picturesque harbour is St. Nicholas Chapel (now a lighthouse—St. Nicholas being the mariners' patron saint) on the Lantern Rock. Close by is the Capstone with its promenade.

Public parks include Victoria Pleasure Grounds, Hillsborough Hill, the Cairn (to the south of the railway station), Bicclescombe Park (tennis courts), St. James's Park (overlooking the harbour). There are numerous sea-bathing places, including Raparee Cove, the Turnels and Hele Beaches, and a covered swimming bath.

Ilfracombe has a great variety of excellent hotels, shops, restaurants, as well as concert halls, cinemas, a museum of natural history, and numerous churches. During the summer there are steamer services to and from Bristol and the Welsh coast, as well as to the adjacent North Devon resorts.

There is an 18-hole golf course at West Haggington, tennis courts and bowling greens.

IVYBRIDGE. A small town on the Erme, 10 miles E. of Plymouth.

There are tennis courts here.

LYDFORD, for a time alleged capital of England, on the edge of Dartmoor, *c.* 20 miles N. of Plymouth.

Lydford Gorge here, two miles in length, is a well-known beauty spot, and, of the numerous waterfalls close by, Lydford Cascade and Kitt's Steps are the most picturesque. The ruins of Lydford Castle, once a Stannary prison of infamous repute under Edward III, lie near Lydford.

Good Books about Devon

HIGHWAYS AND BYWAYS IN DEVON AND CORNWALL. Arthur H. Norway.
IN SEARCH OF ENGLAND. H. V. Morton.
MY NATIVE DEVON. J. W. Fortescue.
VICTORIA COUNTY HISTORY. William Page.
DEVON: ITS MOORLANDS, STREAMS AND COASTS. Lady Rosalind Northcote.
A BOOK OF DEVON. S. Baring-Gould.
TRADITIONS, LEGENDS, SUPERSTITIONS AND SKETCHES OF DEVONSHIRE. Mrs. Anna E. Bray.
FOLK RHYMES OF DEVON. W. Crossing.
LORNA DOONE. R. D. Blackmore.
WESTWARD HO! Charles Kingsley.
THE WESTCOTES. Sir A. T. Quiller-Couch.
MY LADY OF THE MOOR. John Oxenham.
THE FARMER'S WIFE. Eden Philpotts.
DEVONSHIRE CREAM. Eden Philpotts.
YELLOW SANDS. Eden Philpotts.
LITERARY LANDMARKS OF DEVON AND CORNWALL. R. T. Hopkins.

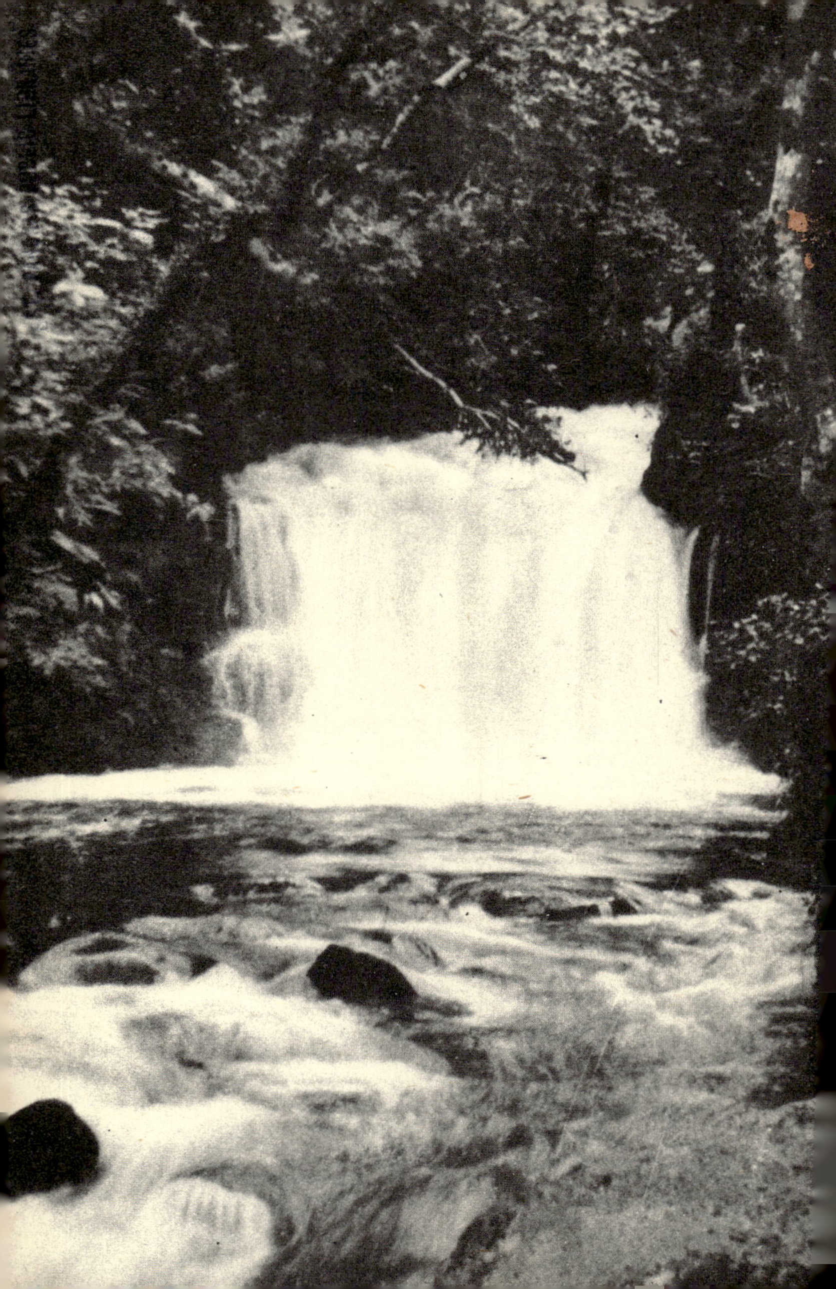

Lynmouth (from an old copper Engraving).

LYNMOUTH *and* LYNTON

LYNMOUTH. A popular and beautiful resort on the north coast, at the confluence of the East and West Lyn, *c.* 16 miles NE. of Barnstaple, with cliff and valley scenery of the most romantic order.

Watersmeet, the Valley of Rocks, Woody Bay, Coombe Martin, Glenthorne, Brendon Valley and Dunkery Beacon are within walking distance. There is a wide choice of excellent hotels, boarding-houses, cafés and shops.

LYNTON. A romantic, unspoiled resort and walking centre on the north coast, adjacent to Lynmouth, *c.* 15 miles NE. of Barnstaple. Lee Abbey, now an hotel, was formerly residence of the Wichehalse family.

There are tennis courts, bowling greens, local trout fishing and numerous hotels and boarding-houses.

MODBURY. A small market town *c.* 13 miles ESE. of Plymouth.

A Knack! A Knack!

Well cut! Well bound! Well shocked! In parts of Devonshire a 'knack' or curious figure was made from twisted sheaves of the last corn cut, carried home with loud acclamation, hung up and kept until the following year. It was most unlucky to part with the 'knack.'

Witches in Devonshire

"EVERY old woman with a wrinkled face, a furr'd brow, a hairy lip, a gobber tooth, a squint eye, a squeaking voice, or a scolding tongue, having a ragged coate upon her back, a skull-cap on her head, a spindle in her hand, and a Dog or Cat by her side, is not only suspected but pronounced for a witch," wrote John Gaule in 1646.

Most extraordinary is the case of Temperance Lloyd of Bideford. Here the symptom of the afflicted—a Mrs. Grace Thomas—was that of 'sticking and pricking Pains as if Pins and Awls had been thrust into her body.' One Elizabeth Eastcheap supplied corroborative evidence of seeing Mrs. Thomas's knee punctured in nine places with a thorn.

Temperance was thereupon approached, and readily admitted that she had a piece of leather full of venom and sorcery, which she had pricked nine times. Not content with this she had entered Thomas Eastcheap's shop in the guise of a grey cat and seized a 'puppit or child's baby.' This she had later pricked all over with pins to encompass the death of Mrs. Grace Thomas.

The doll was not to be found, although Temperance admitted the disguise and the theft, but announced that her Master, the Devil, would tear her to pieces if she gave away the whereabouts of the 'puppit.' The unfortunate witch was by no means slow to tell of further misdemeanours, which included sending a Black Man in the shape of a magpie to afflict the already pain-racked Grace, pinching her, bringing about the death twelve years before of William Herbert, and three years before of Anne Fellows, squeezing another woman until she expired, and hunting with the Devil, the latter disguised as a hound.

She had not, however, ridden on a cow over an arm of the sea, nor bewitched ships nor boats, nor done any children to death.

Remarkable also is the tale of the old dame who, having formed an unholy alliance with the Devil, found that her capacity for turning into a hare could be put to commercial ends. Her grandson was enlisted as an accomplice. He informed the sportsmen of the neighbourhood of the hare's presence in a certain copse, and was given a silver coin for his pains.

During one particularly close pursuit, the lad, unable to contain his enthusiasm, yelled: "Run, Granny, run!" Granny ran to the safety of her cottage. The huntsmen broke down the door, and found the dame with the marks of the dogs' teeth upon her.

She was pardoned, but could not long withdraw from the service of her Satanic master, and was eventually executed.

A Stream near its Source in Dartmoor.

MOLTON. 1. **North Molton,** on the wooded valley of the Mole, *c.* 13 miles E. of Barnstaple.

Copper, iron, lead, silver and gold were formerly mined in the neighbourhood. Here is Court Hall, seat of the Bampfylde family, to whom there are monuments in the church, which has a clerestoried nave. Celebrated North Devon cattle herds are bred here.

2. **South Molton,** an old market town on the Mole, *c.* 12 miles ESE. of Barnstaple.

There are good fishing facilities, and the progressive local council have plans for considerable improvements and extensions which should make this town, lying amid some of the finest scenery in Devon, a favourite centre for visitors to the south-west country.

The Weather Prophet

WHEN Hey Tor wears a hood
Manaton folk may expect no good.

Mount Edgcumbe smoking a cigar,
Rainy weather is not far.

Lundy high, sign of dry,
Lundy plain, sign of rain,
Lundy low, sign of snow.

MORETONHAMPSTEAD.

A market town on the edge of Dartmoor, *c.* 10 miles WSW. of Exeter. Arcaded almshouses here date from 1637.

There are tennis courts and a bathing pool, and the town is an excellent walking centre. 'The Sentry,' an open space with a children's playground, commands good views of the country around.

Some 3 miles to the north-west is Fingle Bridge, on the Teign, amid exceptional scenery, as well as Cranbrook and Wooston Castles, two prehistoric camps overlooking the Teign.

NEWTON ABBOT. A pleasant market town and railway junction on the Teign, *c.* 6 miles NW. of Torquay. Near

the town are the Jacobean Forde House, one-time residence of the Courtenays, and Bradley Manor (fifteenth-century).

There are tennis courts, a public bowling green, an open-air bathing pool, and an important market on Wednesdays. Trout fishing is available in the Teign and other streams near-by, and there is an 18-hole golf course at Stover.

NORTHAM, *c.* 7 miles WSW. of Barnstaple, near Westward Ho! famous for its golf course. Burrough House here has been rebuilt since Kingsley's Amyas Leigh (*see* Westward Ho!) was supposed to live in it. The Pebble Ridge, a natural barrier 2 miles long, is on the seaward side of Northam Burrows, a wide area of waste and pasture land.

Old Almshouses at Moretonhampstead.

Above: Old Print of the magnificent Church at Ottery St. Mary.
Below: The Stocks, Ottery St. Mary.

OKEHAMPTON, or OAK-HAMPTON, an excellent walking and touring centre, and a market town on the fringe of Dartmoor, *c.* 22 miles W. of Exeter.

The picturesque ruins of Okehampton Castle, of pre-Conquest origin, overlook the West Okement Valley and belong to the town.

There is local trout fishing on the Okement, an 18-hole golf course, tennis courts, bowling green, and a swimming bath.

OTTERY ST. MARY. A lovely little town on the Otter, birthplace of the poet Coleridge, *c.* 14 miles ENE. of Exeter.

Its church, perhaps the finest in Devon, has transeptal towers resembling the Norman ones at Exeter

Cathedral, a curious old 'seasonal' clock, a stone reredos with canopied niches, a Lady Chapel with remarkable stone screen, and excellent fan tracery in the Dorset aisle. The church had formerly a whistling weather-cock and still has a seagull-like lectern.

shops, c. 3 miles W. of Torquay.

Its fine red sandstone church of St. John the Baptist has a fifteenth-century chantry screen and a Norman west door.

Near-by is the ruined tower (Cover-

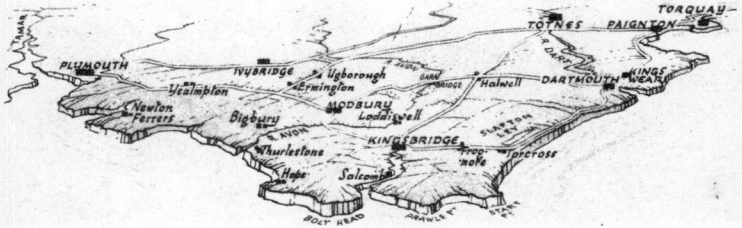

There is good fishing in the Otter here. Near the town is the Tudor Cadhay House (a farm).

PAIGNTON. A pleasant resort unexcelled for safe sea-bathing and boating, with first-class hotels, restaurants and

dale's tower—from the bishop Miles Coverdale, translator of the Bible, who lived here) of what was once a palace of the bishops of Exeter.

There is a good public library, several cinemas, concert halls, an 18-hole golf course (Torbay), and bowling greens.

Plymouth of long ago (from an engraving).

PLYMOUTH

Devon's Romantic Seaport and Naval Base

A LARGE seaport on the south coast, on the estuary of the Plym and Tamar, consisting of the united towns of Plymouth, Devonport and Stonehouse.

Historically it saw the Black Prince sail for France and Crécy with three hundred ships, the comings and goings of the Elizabethan adventurers, Drake, Raleigh, Frobisher and Hawkins, and the departure of the *Mayflower* in 1620 (to found New Plymouth in the New World).

Plymouth Hoe, where Drake received the news of the Armada, overlooks Plymouth Sound, and has near it part of the old Eddystone Lighthouse built by Smeaton. (The Eddystone Lighthouse stands on a dangerous reef some 14 miles S. of the port.) Plymouth Breakwater, 2½ miles from the Hoe, was commenced in 1812.

Buildings.—In the city centre is the ancient Pryston House, formerly a priest's lodging. Enemy bombardment destroyed many fine buildings during the world war (1939–45). Raids were frequent and heavy.

STONEHOUSE contains the Royal Naval Hospital, the Marine Barracks and a naval victualling yard. There are remains of the ancient Stonehouse Manor here and an old tower on Devil's Point.

A fine old House in Plymouth.

Devonport in Days of Sail.

DEVONPORT (formerly *Plymouth Dock*) has naval barracks, an extensive dockyard and a memorial to Scott, the Antarctic explorer.

Plymouth has a good bus service, a fine city museum and art gallery, public libraries, a covered market (town centre), fish market (Sutton Harbour), Astor Institute with its concert hall, and several public parks.

To the visitor Plymouth offers excellent pleasure-steamer cruises up the rivers and along the coast, very good sailing, tennis courts, bowling greens, an attractive regatta, an aquarium, hotels, shops and restaurants.

Excellent sea-fishing is obtainable locally and there are three yacht clubs.

PRINCETOWN (named from George IV when Prince of Wales), in a bleak part of Dartmoor, *c.* 15 miles NE. of Plymouth.

Dartmoor prison was for French captives of the Napoleonic Wars and later for Americans, becoming a convict prison in 1850.

Some trout fishing is available in the headstreams of the Dart and Plym here.

SALCOMBE (sawl'com). A seaside resort and small seaport with bathing, fishing, sailing and golfing facilities, at the mouth of Salcombe estuary, *c.* 20 miles SE. of Plymouth.

Oranges and citrous fruits grow in the open here. It is connected by motor bus and motor boat with Kingsbridge, and there are ferries to Portlemouth.

Salcombe Castle, erected by Henry VIII, stands in ruinous state on a peninsular rock at the harbour entrance. It was the last stronghold of the Royalists in Devon during the

Civil War, and was blockaded for four months in 1646.

St. Peter the Great, one of the largest ships of the Spanish Armada, was wrecked at Hope Cove, 4 miles to the west.

There are tennis courts, a yacht club, a sailing club, and an annual regatta is held in August.

Salcombe claims to have the highest number of hours of sunshine of any place in the British Isles. Winter lays its hand lightly on this beautiful little town.

SEATON.

A seaside resort at the mouth of the Axe, *c.* 20 miles E. of Exeter, with excellent cliff scenery—Haven Cliff, White Cliff, etc.—bathing and trout fishing. Garnets, beryls, chalcedony, jasper, cornelians, agate and other attractive stones are found in the neighbourhood, especially on the beaches.

There are numerous excellent hotels and boarding-houses. Riding lessons are available at the hunting stables, and there are bowling greens, tennis courts, and a golf course.

SIDMOUTH.

A health resort, walking, sea-fishing and bathing centre, at the mouth of the Sid, *c.* 14 miles ESE. of Exeter.

There is a cricket club, an 18-hole golf course, tennis courts, putting and bowling greens, as well as a concert hall, theatre, two cinemas, and numerous first-class hotels and shops. To the south-west is the picturesque Ladram Bay.

STONEHOUSE. *See* PLYMOUTH.

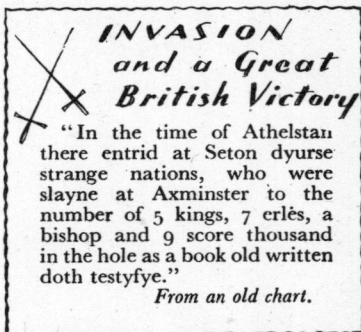

INVASION and a Great British Victory

"In the time of Athelstan there entrid at Seton dyurse strange nations, who were slayne at Axminster to the number of 5 kings, 7 erlès, a bishop and 9 score thousand in the hole as a book old written doth testyfye."

From an old chart.

TAMERTON FOLIOT (from the Foliot family who once resided at Warleigh mansion here), a picturesque but decayed market town at the head of an arm of the Tamar estuary, *c.* 5 miles N. of Plymouth.

TAVISTOCK.

An interesting borough on the western fringe of Dartmoor, on the Tavy, *c.* 15 miles N. of Plymouth, a good centre for visits to Dartmoor.

Remains of a famous tenth-century Benedictine abbey may be seen in the structure of the Bedford hotel (fine vaulted porch—original entrance to the abbey church), vicarage grounds (two gateways), the Unitarian Chapel (the frater) and the parish church (fragment of the monks' lavatory).

There is an 18-hole golf course, good local stream fishing for trout, tennis and bowling facilities in the 'Meadows', and a public swimming bath.

Some distance to the W. are Morwell Rocks (magnificent river scenery on the Tamar), and the fifteenth-century Morwell House, former country residence of the Abbots of Tavistock.

Top: *Seaton Promenade.*   *Below*: *Salcombe Hill near Sidmouth.*

Ladram Bay near Sidmouth.

Teignmouth (from an engraving after Turner).

TEIGNMOUTH (tin'mouth). A seaport on the Teign estuary, where it enters the sea, *c.* 7 miles N. of Torquay.

Teignmouth has excellent bathing, boating, sea-fishing, tennis and bowling and an 18-hole golf course. It has a fine selection of hotels, boarding-houses, and shops, and a good sea-front promenade ('the Den'). Orchestral concerts and dances are held in the Den Pavilions.

To the north-east there is notable red cliff scenery around the Parson and Clerk promontory.

A bridge joins Teignmouth to Shaldon (also worth a visit) on the opposite side of the Teign estuary.

TIVERTON. A market town above the confluence of the Exe and the Loman, *c.* 13 miles N. of Exeter.

It has the interesting church of St. Peter (*see* particularly Greenways Chapel), sixteenth-century almshouses and remains of a castle of the Courtenays.

There is a library, a covered market, and lace manufactures. Recreational facilities include an 18-hole golf course, Cumberland turf and other bowling greens, and some local shooting and fishing.

TOPSHAM. A town on the Exe, *c.* 5 miles SE. of Exeter.

There are interesting old Dutch gabled houses well worth examination, and tennis courts.

Stalactites in Kent's Cavern, Torquay.

Torquay Harbour.

TORQUAY

The Outstanding Resort of England's South Coast Riviera

THIS borough and watering-place of great renown, on a magnificent undulating site overlooking Tor Bay, lies *c.* 23 miles S. of Exeter.

Anstey's Cove (bathing), Bishop's Walk, Marine Drive (magnificent views) lie on the coast to the east of the town, Babbacombe (fine downs, beaches and cliff scenery), St. Mary-church to the north-east and Cockington (*see* article) to the west.

The extensive Kent's Cavern has yielded valuable remains of pre-historic men and of cave animals.

The Premonstratensian Torre Abbey was founded at the end of the twelfth century; its remains include part of the presbytery, transepts, west doorway and windows of the chapter house, and the monastic Tithe Barn (known locally as 'the Spanish Barn').

The fourteenth-century St. Saviour's Church should be visited.

The Princess Pier adjoins Princess Gardens, with its palm trees and fountain, and at the opposite end of the gardens is the Pavilion where the municipal orchestra performs and theatrical productions are featured each week. The Marine Spa has a sun lounge, large swimming baths, and fine medical sections for spa treatments.

There is a covered market, a public library, a museum (containing many objects from Kent's Cavern, and a good library), as well as a large number of first-class hotels and

Gardens in Torquay.

boarding-houses, cafés, shops, two concert halls, and six cinemas.

Torquay has yacht clubs, a cricket club, an 18-hole golf course, tennis courts, bowling greens, ample facilities for sea-bathing, fishing, boating, motor-boat and steamer trips in Torbay and around the neighbouring coast.

At the end of last century Torquay was described as follows: "This town . . . was a mere fishing village prior to the great wars with France. It became the residence of numerous families connected with the Channel Fleet under Lord St. Vincent. It attracted extensive notice, through them, for the beauty of its views, and its general amenities for seaside residence and seaside bathing. It rose rapidly into importance as a resort of invalids, sea-bathers and summer rusticators, and ranks now as one of the very finest watering-places in the world. It stands partly in sheltered valleys, partly in breezy hills, covers more ground in proportion to its population than any other town in England." The elements of this description are even more true of Torquay to-day. Successive visits by royalty and nobility have lent this delightful resort a dignity and atmosphere which is difficult to imagine outside of the Mediterranean coast.

Although Torquay is lacking in buildings and associations of historical interest, it lies, nevertheless, in an area which, for the sheer richness and diversity of its architecture, would be difficult to equal in the southern counties. Exeter and its ecclesiastical magnificence is accessible with ease; the quaint Brixham and its old-world harbour are within walking distance; Totnes, with its gabled houses and old gateways, is near at hand. Cockington village lies administratively within Torquay, while Dartmoor, with its stone rows and barrows, lies to the north-west.

Brixham Fishing Boats in Torquay Harbour.

SEA FISHING off the Devon Coast

APPLEDORE. In the late summer bass are obtainable in Bideford Bay.

BUDLEIGH SALTERTON. Between Budleigh Salterton and Sidmouth mackerel can often be taken, and whiting of good size are caught in some seasons. Dabs are found on the sandy river bars, while pollack and bass are present off the mouth of the Otter.

Rag-worms and mussels are to be had locally for bait.

BRIXHAM. Excellent fishing is available along the steep coast here. Pollack and bass can be taken on rag-worm from a boat or from the rocks. Conger are caught near Berry Head.

CLOVELLY. Bass and pollack fishing is good along the coast here, and also much practised round Lundy Island.

DARTMOUTH. Near the Mewstone and other rocks shoals of bass and pollack are to be found. Whiting and mackerel fishing is also obtainable locally, the former being taken chiefly in the late summer.

DAWLISH. There is good sea fishing for pollack, mackerel and dabs here. Sand-worms for bait can be got on the beach.

EXMOUTH. Mackerel fishing is very popular off the coast. Good mussels for bait are to be had in the harbour. Whiffing for bass is also prac-tised; this consists of trolling in a tideway with a dead sand eel for bait. The usual practice is to bring the hook out at the tail of the eel.

HARTLAND POINT. There is excellent bass fishing with a spinning red eel.

ILFRACOMBE. Bass, pollack and dabs are caught from boats here.

PLYMOUTH. Cawsand Bay affords good fishing for pout, whiting and dabs, while off Penlee Point are to be found mackerel, bass and pollack.

Whiting, cod, haddock, bream and gurnards are found in quantities about 10 miles outside Plymouth, and for this fishing the services of a good boatman are required.

SALCOMBE. With live sand-eel bait mullet and bass are taken off the coast here.

SEATON. There is bass fishing near Axmouth Harbour.

SIDMOUTH. Good sea fishing of many varieties is available. Shallow coasts here cause dangerous surf when there is a breeze.

TEIGNMOUTH. Excellent bass fishing was formerly obtainable here. Now mackerel, pollack and dab fishing are chiefly practised.

TORQUAY. Good pollack fishing is to be had, and the usual supply of mackerel and dabs. Occasionally whiting are present in great quantities.

The Guildhall in Totnes.

GREAT TORRINGTON. A pleasant, ancient town above the Torridge, *c.* 10 miles SSW. of Barnstaple. On Castle Hill, overlooking the river, was formerly a castle, of which the remains are used as a school. Great Torrington has good public tennis courts and a cinema, and trout fishing is obtainable in the Torridge.

The charter granted in 1554 includes the right to hold fairs in May and October; the former has attained renown for its Maypole and Furry Dances in the streets and square.

During the Civil Wars two hundred Royalist prisoners were accidentally blown up in the church when the stores of gunpowder there exploded.

Little Torrington village lies 3 miles to the south.

TOTNES (tot'nes). A market town on the Dart, *c.* 10 miles WSW. of Torquay.

Anciently a walled town, Totnes had four gates, two of which remain—the east and the north gates—the former spanning the colonnaded High Street with its Elizabethan houses. There are vestiges of the keep and moat of Totnes Castle (surrounded by pleasant grounds). The church has a magnificent fifteenth-century stone screen.

Totnes has a public library, as well as first-class tennis courts and bowling green, and trout fishing on the Dart, while steamers sail between the town and Dartmouth in the summer.

45

WESTWARD HO! A resort on the north coast, named from Charles Kingsley's book, *c.* 4 miles NW. of Bideford. There is a famous 18-hole golf course here (Royal North Devon). The special handbook on the course, by Bernard Darwin, will shortly be obtainable again from the secretary.

Kipling's novel *Stalky and Co.*, is based on the author's own schooldays here.

The ancient East Gate to the town of Totnes.

The fame of Sir Francis Drake

TRADITION in Devonshire was for long busy with the exploits of Sir Francis Drake. The remarkable Elizabethan adventurer was born about 1540 in a tiny cottage, now demolished, in Crowndale, near Tavistock.

At the time when witchcraft was rampant it was not surprising that the 'old warrior' was popularly believed to be invested with supernatural powers. For long the historic incident of the game of bowls on Plymouth Hoe was rendered even more colourful by the following legend attaching to it:

The Armada was reported to the players, who all showed their complete unconcern. The game finished, Sir Francis obtained a hatchet and a large balk of timber. The latter he cut into small sections, which were thrown by his own hand into the sea. From every block arose a fire ship, and history records more accurately the immense damage and confusion which these flaming vessels wrought upon the luckless Spanish fleet.

One of Drake's marauding expeditions having lasted the somewhat protracted length of seven years, his good lady, justifiably assuming that her sailor was safe in Davy Jones's locker, decided to take unto herself another husband. The bridegroom was selected and

the nuptial ceremony about to begin, when one of Drake's informant sprites carried the distressing news to his master. Sir Francis in great rage shot off a cannon ball with such velocity and accuracy, that it speeded over countless leagues of ocean and fell with a loud explosion beside the church altar, between the lady and her intended husband. "It is the signal from Drake," she said. "He is alive, and I am still a wife. There must be neither troth nor ring between thee and me!"

In the sixteenth century many country folks believed that the world consisted of two parallel planes, and that a great gulf existed between the upper and lower levels. Sir Francis was popularly reputed to have 'shot the gulf,' plunging his ship safely over the upper edge to the waters beneath. It is recorded that in Oxford a somewhat unsophisticated guide, indicating an old picture of the Admiral, pistol in hand, described him as about to 'shoot the gulf.'

Sailing in the southern seas Drake is said to have questioned a cabin boy of remarkable ability on his knowledge of geography. The boy gave him the location of the ship immediately as antipodal to Barton Place (now Buckland Abbey), the Admiral's mansion in Devonshire. Later the question was again asked, and the boy gave London Bridge as their antipodes.

"Hast thou too, a devil?" Drake is alleged to have exclaimed. "If I let thee live there will be one a greater man than I am in the world." The unfortunate youth was thereupon thrown overboard.

Such stories possibly had their origin in the Spaniards' linking up of Drake with the Devil. Likely enough such necromantic associations became food for gossip among the English Catholics, and the stories gained credence from the women folk for their romantic nature.

The actual facts of the life of this astounding seaman are striking enough. He served a naval apprenticeship, and soon was conversant with the waters of the Spanish Main. He commanded the *Judeth* in Hawkins' ill-fated expedition of 1567.

Revenge in his heart, he landed at Nombre de Dios in May, 1572 with a handful of men, but was so severely wounded that he was compelled to withdraw, leaving his loot behind him. In the same year, he reached Porto Bello, and gazed upon the South Seas, beseeching "Almighty God of his goodness to give him life and leave to sail once in an English ship in that sea!" When Drake landed at Plymouth in 1573 he was already a popular hero.

He did indeed enter the Pacific in 1578 in the *Golden Hind*. Failing to find his way back into the familiar waters of the Atlantic, he struck across the vast Pacific, refitted in Java after over two months desperate sailing, and, having rounded the Cape of Good Hope, arrived in England, to the confusion of many and the astonishment of all, in 1580.

The Queen, playing a difficult part, knighted her Admiral in 1581, and he continued to harry the Dons with greater verve than ever before. This culminated in two remarkable events.

The first was the destruction of thirty-three ships of the Spanish fleet in Cadiz Harbour in 1587. The second was the decisive part which Sir Francis played in the elimination of the Spanish Armada.

Drake died off Porto Bello, the scene of his earlier exploit, in 1596.

Villages
&
Natural
Beauty Spots

Okehampton · Widecombe · Newsteignton

Frithelstock Priory.

ABBOT'S BICKINGTON, on the Torridge, *c.* 18 miles SW. of Barnstaple, with interesting ancient glass in the chancel windows of its church.

ABBOTSHAM, *c.* 10 miles WSW. of Barnstaple, has a church with fine-toned bells and good carving on its old bench ends.

ABBOTSKERSWELL, *c.* 7 miles NW. of Torquay, in an excellent cider district, has an ancient church and church house. Interesting pottery and wrought iron have been made near-by.

ABBOT'S WAY. An ancient track, still traceable, across Dartmoor, from Buckfastleigh to Tavistock.

ALLINGTON, EAST, *c.* 15 miles SW. of Torquay, has Fallapit, a mansion in the Elizabethan style, former seat of the Fortescues, whose arms

and brasses may be seen in the interesting Perpendicular church here.

ALPHINGTON, on the Exe, *c.* 2 miles S. of Exeter. The church of St. Michael has a round Norman font carved with figures and scroll-work, and the ancient wayside Alphington Cross stands near-by.

ALVINGTON, WEST, *c.* 18 miles SW. of Torquay. Portions of the mansion of Bowringslea, former seat of the Bowrings and Ilberts, are of the thirteenth century. It has elaborate Jacobean wood-carving, rich ceilings and valuable pictures. All Saints Church is worth a visit.

ALWINGTON, *c.* 12 miles SW. of Barnstaple, contains Portledge House, with old carved oak and portraits of the Coffin family, of whom it is the seat.

ARLINGTON, *c.* 7 miles NE. of

Barnstaple, has the manor house of Arlington Court.

ASHCOMBE, *c.* 11 miles S. of Exeter, has a church with early Flemish glass in the east window, and (near the village) Mamhead Obelisk (1742: originally a guide to vessels at sea).

ASHFORD, on the Taw, *c.* 3 miles NW. of Barnstaple. The altar, pulpit, and pews in the modern church are old and interesting.

ASHPRINGTON, *c.* 8 miles SW. of Torquay, has the ancient manor house of Painsford, one-time possession of the Somaster and Courtenay families. Sharpham House, originally belonging to the Winards, has interesting grounds containing a heronry and a colossal elm-tree.

ASHTON, *c.* 8 miles SW. of Exeter, has a picturesque seventeenth-century bridge over the Teign. Near Ashton was the former seat of the Chudleighs, Place Barton. The church has ancient painted screens and good bench ends.

ATHERINGTON, 8 miles SSE. of Barnstaple, has a fascinating church with ancient and richly carved oak screens and bench ends, a rood loft (the only one in Devon), and fine old glass of the fifteenth century.

AVETON GIFFORD (aw'ton ji'ferd), *c.* 17 miles ESE. of Plymouth, near the Avon, has a fine old church.

AVON (awn). A good salmon river, rising in Dartmoor and flowing to the south coast at Bigbury Bay.

AWLISCOMBE ('owlescombe' named from its numerous owls or from a family of that name), *c.* 16 miles ENE. of Exeter, is near Hembury Fort, an ancient camp with clearly discernible ramparts. The old church at Awliscombe has a magnificent stone screen.

AXE. A river rising in Dorset, flowing through Axminster to the south coast at Seaton.

BABBACOMBE. *See* TORQUAY.

BEER. A large and attractive fishing village, once a smugglers' stronghold, in a deep valley on the south coast, *c.* 20 miles E. of Exeter. It is a lace-making centre (Honiton style) and has large freestone quarries from which the material for Exeter cathedral was chiefly furnished. To the north-west is Bovey House (partly Norman) and to the south-west the precipitous Beer Head.

BELSTONE, admirably situated on the fringe of Dartmoor, near the Taw, *c.* 18 miles W. of Exeter. Near it are two stone circles and a menhir, relics of prehistoric occupation.

There is local trout fishing here.

BERRYNARBOR, near the north coast, *c.* 10 miles N. of Barnstaple, has a manor house built in the reign of Edward IV, Watermouth Castle (1825), and an ancient church.

BERRY POMEROY, on the Dart, *c.* 7 miles WSW. of Torquay, has a castle (1 mile to the north-east),

Devonshire Cream

Allow milk to stand in a pan for several hours. Then heat extremely slowly until small rings are formed on the surface (180 F.). The pan should be put in a cool place for twenty-four hours, and the cream then skimmed off.

Entrance Gateway of Berry Pomeroy Castle.

Beer Head.

now in ruins, erected by Ralph de Pomeroy, allegedly the recipient of the manor from William the Conqueror, and a church (fifteenth-century) with a fine rood screen.

BICKLEIGH. 1. Picturesquely situated near the Plym, overlooked by the Dewerstone Crags, *c.* 6 miles N. of Plymouth.

2. On the Exe, *c.* 12 miles N. of Exeter, the burial-place of the notorious Bampfylde Moore Carew, one-time 'King of the Gipsies' and naval adventurer, whose parents lived at Bickleigh Court here.

BIGBURY–ON–SEA, *c.* 15 miles ESE. of Plymouth, has a fine view of Bigbury Bay. There is an 18-hole golf course here.

BISHOP'S NYMPTON, near the Mole, *c.* 14 miles ESE. of Barnstaple, in an unspoiled hilly district, has a church with a fine Perpendicular tower.

BISHOP'S TAWTON, on the Taw, *c.* 3 miles SSE. of Barnstaple. Hall mansion near-by has magnificent woodwork in its old banqueting hall.

BISHOP'S TEIGNTON (tin'ton), *c.* 8 miles N. of Torquay, has a remarkable Norman tympanum on the south wall of its church with figures representing the Adoration. There are bowling greens here.

BLACKAWTON, *c.* 12 miles SW. of Torquay, has ancient paintings on the rood screen of its interesting old church.

BOLT HEAD. A headland (430 feet) on the south coast, *c.* 20 miles ESE. of Plymouth. Beneath it are Bull's Hole and Stair Hole Caverns.

BOVEY (buv'i). **1. North Bovey,** on the edge of Dartmoor, *c.* 11 miles WSW. of Exeter, has several ancient crosses, notably one on the village green, while to the west near Grims-

The ancient Granite Cross at North Bovey.

pound are prehistoric circles and barrows. There is an 18-hole golf course here.

2. Bovey Tracey, *c.* 10 miles SSW. of Exeter, commands good views of Dartmoor, and has an old gateway ('Cromwell's Arch').

BRADNINCH, formerly an ancient borough, *c.* 8 miles NE. of Exeter, has a chancel screen of great beauty (fifteenth - century) in its church, with paintings of the Annunciation and the Salutation as well as figures of saints, doctors and judges. It has an old Manor House.

BRADSTONE, near the Tamar, *c.* 20 miles NNW. of Plymouth, has an old mansion, for long seat of the Cloberry family, with a picturesque gate-house and a stone, alleged execution block of St. Nonna the martyr.

BRADWORTHY, *c.* 20 miles SW. of Barnstaple, has a Jacobean pulpit in its church.

BRANSCOMBE, on the south coast, *c.* 18 miles E. of Exeter, amid wild and fascinating scenery, with good bathing facilities near-by. Its church shows Saxon masonry.

BRATTON CLOVELLY, *c.* 25 miles N. of Plymouth, probable birthplace of Henry de Bracton, the 'Father of English Law,' has a thirteenth and fourteenth-century church.

BRAUNTON ('Brannock's town' —from its founder, St. Brannock), 6 miles WNW. of Barnstaple, alleged to have been anciently an important place.

BRENDON. A picturesque village on the Somerset border, near the north coast, *c.* 14 miles NE. of Barnstaple, with trout fishing in the neighbouring streams.

BRENT, SOUTH, on the Avon, *c.* 16 miles ENE. of Plymouth, overlooked by a tor, has near it prehistoric hut circles, stone crosses and a cromlech.

BRENTOR, *c.* 16 miles N. of Plymouth, has an Early English church on the summit of a conspicuous hill.

BRIDESTOWE (brid'es-to), *c.* 23 miles NNE. of Plymouth, has Leawood, a modern mansion with a fine park, and remains of the old house. Bidlake near-by is Elizabethan in style. The churchyard has an unusual Norman gateway and the church interesting old bench ends.

There is local trout fishing.

BRIDFORD, *c.* 8 miles SW. of Exeter, has in its church a fine oak screen dated 1508 with the pomegranate of Aragon and paintings upon it, some mediæval glass, and an interesting rood screen.

BRIXTON, *c.* 5 miles ESE. of Plymouth, has near it the remains of Hareston manor house and Spriddlestone, anciently a seat of the Fortescues, now a farm house.

BROADCLYST (brawd'clist), *c.* 7 miles NE. of Exeter. Killerton Park, seat of the Aclands, is a Georgian mansion with interesting, well-wooded grounds between the rivers Culm and Clyst (open to the public on Sunday afternoons).

BROADHEMBURY, *c.* 16 miles NE. of Exeter, has a tablet in its church commemorating Toplady, author of *Rock of Ages*, one-time vicar here. The church shows Tudor decoration on its roof and has interesting old bells. Near-by is Hembury Fort, a notable prehistoric earthwork, and the mansion of Hembury Fort house.

BROADHEMPSTON, *c.* 12 miles W. of Torquay, has a church, rebuilt in 1402, with an ancient screen and fragmentary mediæval glass, bearing the arms of Barnhouse and Rowe.

Branscombe from the East.

Main Roads ━━━━
[divided into
5 mile sections thus]
Secondary Roads ━━━━
Lanes & footpaths ━━━━

W — S — E

Lynmo
Lynton
Ilfracombe   Combe
                  martin
Woolocombe
Saunton
Braunton   BARNSTAPLE   North
                                        Molton
Appledore   South Molton
Westward Ho!   Instow
        Northam   BIDEFORD   Bishops Ny.
Hartland   Clovelly
                    St.   Kings
                  Torrington   Nympton
Welcombe   Chulmleigh
        Bradworthy   Eggesfora
                    Petrockstow
            Shebbear
BUDE   Stratton   Hatherleigh
        Holsworthy   Credito
                                    Okehampton
                Bratton Clovelly
                Bridestowe   High   Drewsteig
                            Willhaus Gidleigh R.Teig
                    Lifton   Chagford   More
LAUNCESTON   Lydford   Ham
                    Brentor   Mano
                                        Post
                        Marytavy   Bridge
                        Petertavy Two Bridges   Wayto
C   Widecombe Bucki
O   CALLINGTON R.TAMAR   FAVISTOCK
R   Ashi
N   Holne
W   Yelverton Buckfastleigh
A   R.PLYM   TOT
L   SALTASH   Dibi
L   Tamerton   Plympton IVYBRIDGE
        Folio   PLYMOUTH
                                        Modbury
                                        Loddiswe
                    Newland   KING
                    Ferrers Bigbury   -BRID
                        Thurlestone
                                        Sale

MINEHEAD

MOOR

SOMERSET

BRIDGWATER

TAUNTON

Bampton

Burlescombe

TIVERTON

YEOVIL

Cadbury

Cullompton

CHARD

Thorverton

R. EXE

Plymtree

Honiton

AXMINSTER

BRIDPORT

DORSET

Ottery St Mary

Clyst St Mary

Colyton

Seaton Axmouth

LYME REGIS

EXETER

Topsham

Beer

SIDMOUTH

Branscombe

Doddiscomb-sleigh

Budleigh Salterton

Chudleigh

EXMOUTH

Dawlish

TEIGNMOUTH

Newton Abbot

TORQUAY

Paignton

Stoke Gabriel

Dittis-hams

BRIXHAM

Kingswear

DARTMOUTH

Torcross

WALKING & CYCLING MAP of DEVON

Hayes Barton, birthplace of Raleigh.

58

Cottages and Church at Broadhembury.

BRUSHFORD, *c.* 17 miles SSE. of Barnstaple, has an interesting church with a wooden tower and an ancient, well-preserved, wood screen.

There is good local trout fishing.

BUCKERELL, *c.* 15 miles NNE. of Exeter, has near it Deer Park, said to be anciently a royal hunting-box. Part of the oak screen in the church here is very old.

BUCKFAST ABBEY. *See* BUCK-FASTLEIGH.

BUCKLAND BREWER, *c.* 12 miles SW. of Barnstaple. Orleigh, formerly belonging to the Dennys family, is a fine old mansion.

BUCKLAND MONACHO-RUM, *c.* 9 miles N. of Plymouth, has a mansion named Buckland Abbey (formerly a church) containing relics associated with Sir Francis Drake, including a drum. Its church has a Drake chapel, fifteenth-century glass

in the east window, and the tomb of General Elliott (Lord Heathfield), hero of the Siege of Gibraltar (1780-3).

BUDLEIGH, EAST, *c.* 10 miles SE. of Exeter, has near it the Eliza-bethan Hayes Barton, now a farm, birthplace of Sir Walter Raleigh in 1552.

BURLESCOMBE, on the Somerset border, *c.* 20 miles NE. of Exeter, has important associations in its church, and at Ayshford Court (now a farm house) and chapel, with the Ayshford family. At Canons Leigh near-by are the ruins of a Benedictine nunnery founded by Maud, Countess of Devon, in the reign of Henry III.

CADBURY, *c.* 8 miles N. of Exeter, has Cadbury Castle, an ancient camp occupied by Fairfax's army in 1645. Excavations here in 1848 yielded bracelets, Roman coins, and human bones among other things.

CHERITON BISHOP, *c.* 10 miles W. of Exeter, has a church containing parts of an ancient painted screen, and fragmentary mediæval glass. Near it are the manor houses of Medland and Great Fulford, the latter stormed by Fairfax in 1645 during the Civil War.

CHERITON FITZPAINE, *c.* 10 miles N. of Exeter, has almshouses endowed in 1594.

CHITTLEHAMPTON, *c.* 6 miles SE. of Barnstaple, has a magnificent tower on its church which is also notable for its fine timbered roofs. Brightley Park and manor house, anciently seat of the Giffords (monuments in the church should be seen) is now a farm.

CHIVELSTONE, in a secluded valley, *c.* 25 miles SSW. of Torquay. Its church of St. Silvester has an ancient pulpit carved from solid oak, and interesting paintings of saints on its old rood screen.

CHRISTOW, on the Teign, *c.* 7 miles SW. of Exeter, with disused silver and lead mines. There is good fishing here in the river and in the Torquay reservoirs near-by. Canonteign House, a brick mansion, stands in extensive and beautiful grounds.

CHULMLEIGH (chum'li), overlooking the little Dart, *c.* 16 miles SE. of Barnstaple. The church porch has an almost unique Norman or Celtic figure carving of Christ on the Cross, fully clothed. Colleton Manor and Garland (now a farm house), seat of a family of that name, are here.

CHURCHSTOW, *c.* 15 miles SW. of Torquay, overlooks Combe Royal, a Tudor mansion with oranges and citrous fruits growing in its sheltered gardens.

CHURCHSTONE FERRERS, 6 miles SSW. of Torquay, has an 18-hole golf course ('Churston').

CLAYHIDON, *c.* 22 miles NE. of Exeter. Garlandhayes here was once the manor of the Hidon family.

Buried Treasure—

"If Cadbury Castle & Dolbury Hill down delved were, Then Devonshire might plough with a golden coulter and eare with a golden share—"

A Dragon, keeper of the treasure, was alleged to fly nightly between Cadbury Castle and Dolbury Hill—

CLYST HYDON, CLYST ST. GEORGE, CLYST ST. MARY, villages to the east of Exeter, on the Clyst.

COCKINGTON, within Torquay, has an old forge and an interesting Perpendicular church with fragmentary ancient glass and a fifteenth-century pulpit. Cockington Court here was once seat of the Carys.

COFFINSWELL, *c.* 6 miles NNW.

of Torquay, has an ancient manor house and church.

COLATON RALEIGH, *c.* 12 miles ESE. of Exeter. Place Court, an ancient mansion, has associations with Sir Walter Raleigh.

COLEBROOKE, *c.* 12 miles NW. of Exeter, has a fine oak screen and carved bench ends in its church, which has heraldic associations with the Coplestone family, who once owned Coplestone house here. Nearby is the granite Coplestone Cross, some 11 feet high, mentioned in a Saxon document of A.D. 974.

COLERIDGE, or **COLDRIDGE**, on the Taw. *c.* 17 miles NW. of Exeter, has late Gothic screens, ancient glass, and old tiles in its church.

COLYFORD. *See* COLYTON.

COMBE MARTIN, on Combmartin Bay, *c.* 10 miles to the north of Barnstaple, formerly a market and lead and silver mining town, now a village. Its church has a fine tower and good ancient paintings on its screen.

CORNWOOD, *c.* 10 miles ENE. of Plymouth, in the south-west corner of Dartmoor, in the beautiful Yealm vale, at the head of which is the cascaded Hawns and Dendles valley. There is an interesting church in Cornwood and near-by are stone rows, hut circles, and other prehistoric monuments. Slade, Blackford, Fardel, and Wisdom mansions lie in or near the village.

CORNWORTHY, *c.* 7 miles SW. of Torquay, has the gateway and part of a chapel belonging to an Augustinian nunnery, and remains of a Roman encampment.

COUNTESS WEAR, or **COUNTESS WEIR** (so-called from a thirteenth-century attempt by a countess of Devon to obstruct Exeter's

Cockington Village near Torquay.

An old Bridge near Chagford Town.

navigation). A south-eastern suburb of Exeter, with a golf course.

COUNTISBURY, on the north coast, near the Somerset border, *c.* 16 miles NE. of Barnstaple, with attractive coastal scenery and cliff walks. On Oldbarrow Down near-by are the remains of a prehistoric encampment. Glenthorne, a modern mansion, has grounds which are open to the public.

CROCKERN TOR. *See* DARTMOOR.

CRUWYS (crooz) **MORCHARD**, *c.* 15 miles N. of Exeter. Its church has a Georgian screen and adjacent to it is Cruwys Morchard House, seat of the Cruwys family.

CULMSTOCK (cum′stok), *c.* 20 miles NE. of Exeter, on the Culm. In its church there is an interesting stone screen, which now does duty as a reredos, and an old altar cloth.

DALWOOD, *c.* 23 miles ENE. of Exeter, has some mediæval glass in its church.

DART. A river rising in Dartmoor, with two head-streams uniting at the beautiful hamlet of Dartmeet, flows past Buckfast Abbey, through Totnes, Dartmouth, and Kingswear to its rocky estuary on the south coast. It provides good salmon and trout fishing.

DARTINGTON, on the Dart, *c.* 8 miles W. of Torquay, has the old manor of Dartington Hall, dating in part (notably a barn and banqueting hall) from the fourteenth century, for long residence of the Campernownes, now a cultural centre for enlightened rural education and headquarters of the Ballets Jooss.

DARTMOOR. An elevated moorland in the south-west of Devon, notable for its wild scenery, and rich in prehistoric remains. High Willhays (2,039 feet) and Yes Tor (2,029 feet) in the north of the moor are the highest points.

Crockern Tor was the scene of the court of the Stanneries of Devon, and Wistman's Wood consists of small patches of original oak woodland.

DARTMOOR PRISON. *See* PRINCETOWN.

DAWLISH. A pleasant sea-bathing resort on the south coast, *c.* 10 miles SSE. of Exeter, amid picturesque red cliff scenery. There is good sea-fishing for mackerel and pollack, and Dawlish has tennis courts.

DEAN PRIOR, *c.* 14 miles W. of Torquay. Herrick the poet was vicar here for protracted periods from 1629 onwards.

DENBURY, *c.* 8 miles WNW. of Torquay, overlooked by Denbury Down and its earthworks. Denbury church has a sixteenth-century screen brought from Dartington church.

DIPTFORD, *c.* 15 miles WSW. of Torquay. The manor house and buildings of Crabadon Court date from the fifteenth century.

DITTISHAM. A pleasant place on the Dart, *c.* 4 miles N. of Dartmouth, notable for fruit-growing and salmon fishing.

DODDISCOMBLEIGH, *c.* 6 miles SW. of Exeter, with remarkable mediæval window glass in its church.

DOWN, EAST and **WEST.** Two pretty villages, *c.* 8 miles to the north of Barnstaple.

DREWSTEIGNTON (drooztayn'ton), *c.* 12 miles W. of Exeter, near the well-known Fingle Bridge over the Teign. Drewsteignton cromlech, or Spinster's Rock, a Logan stone, Prestonbury and Woostow Castle (two camps), are prehistoric remains here.

DUNCHIDEOCK (dun-chid'ok), *c.* 4 miles SW. of Exeter. Conspicuous

Combe Martin (from an old print).

63

Rocks on Dartmoor.

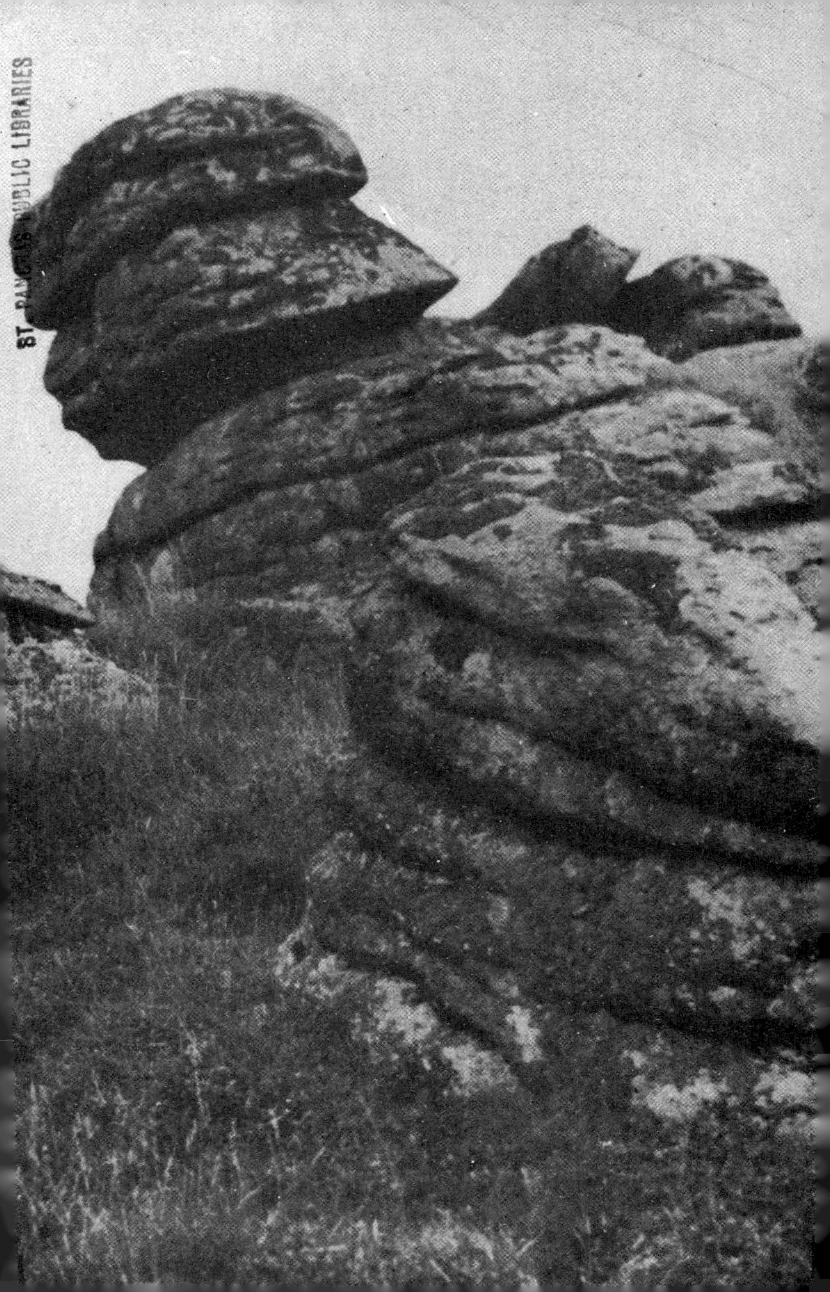

Old Clapper Bridge at Dartmeet.

here on a height is the tower of Haldon Belvedere, a landmark and viewpoint.

DUNKESWELL, *c.* 16 miles NE. of Exeter, has remains of a Cistercian Abbey founded here in the thirteenth century.

DUNSFORD, on the Teign, *c.* 7 miles WSW. of Exeter. The partly Elizabethan Great Fulford house here is the residence of the well-known Fulford family.

DUNTERTON, on the Tamar, *c.* 20 miles NNW. of Plymouth, in an outstandingly beautiful wooded region.

EAST ALLINGTON. *See* ALL. INGTON.

EAST DOWN. *See* DOWN.

EAST OGWELL. *See* OGWELL.

EAST WORLINGTON. *See* WORLINGTON.

RINGERS' RULES at Drewsteignton Church

1. Whoever in this place shall swear,
   6d. shall he pay therefore.
2. He that rings here in his hat,
   3d. shall he pay for that.
3. Who overturns a bell, be sure,
   3d. shall he pay therefore.
4. Who leaves his rope under-feet,
   3d. shall he pay for it.
5. A good ringer and a true heart,
   Will never refuse to stand a quart.
   Who will not to these rules agree,
   Shall not belong to this belfree.

66

EGGESFORD, *c.* 17 miles SSE. of Barnstaple, has notable monuments to the Chichester, Fellowes, and Wallop families in its church.

There is trout fishing in the Taw.

ERME. A river rising in Dartmoor near Erme Head (1,131 feet), flows to Bigbury Bay on the south coast, its upper course rich in prehistoric remains (notably the circles at Erme Pound).

ERME POUND. *See* ERME.

ERMINGTON, *c.* 10 miles E. of Plymouth, has a large Jacobean screen in its church.

EXBOURNE, on the Okement, with good trout fishing, *c.* 22 miles WNW. of Exeter. It has an ancient church.

EXE. A river rising in Exmoor in Somerset, passes Tiverton and Exeter to enter the sea by a long estuary at Exmouth. Its best-known tributaries are the Culm, Creedy and Clyst, and it has notable salmon and trout fishing.

FARWAY, *c.* 18 miles ENE. of Exeter, is overlooked by Farway Down. There are numerous prehistoric remains here, including 'Farway Castle,' an early encampment.

FENITON, *c.* 15 miles ENE. of Exeter, has interesting associations with the Malherbes and Ferrers families, as displayed by heraldry on the capitals of its church pillars. Prehistoric camps in the neighbourhood include Hembury, Woodbury and Dumpton.

FILLEIGH, *c.* 7 miles ESE. of Barnstaple. Castlehill here is the seat of the Fortescues (to whom there are sixteenth-century brasses in the church). The finely wooded park is unfortunately not open to the public.

The Cliffs at Dawlish.

ARCHITECTURE IN
and how to

Norman Style 1050 - 1200

**USE OF THE ROUND ARCH
GENERAL MASSIVENESS OF
DESIGN.**

Early English 1150 - 1300

**POINTED ARCH SUPERSEDES
THE ROUND ARCH — USE OF
"LANCET" HEADED WINDOWS
IN GROUPS.**

DEVON & CORNWALL
understand it

Decorated 1250-1400

DEVELOPMENT OF TRACERIED
WINDOWS. EXCLUSIVE USE
OF POINTED ARCH

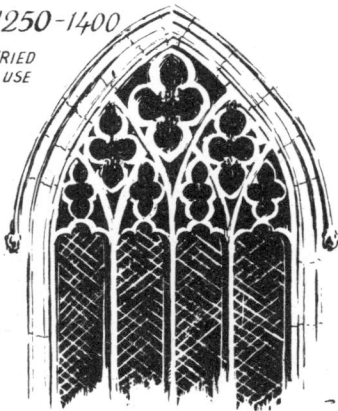

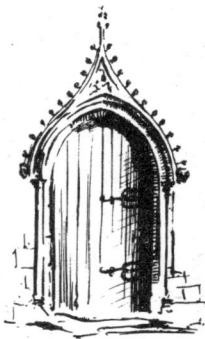

Perpendicular

INSISTENCE ON VERTICAL
LINES IN DESIGN. FLATTER
ARCHES. MORE DELICATE
TRACERY

1350-1500

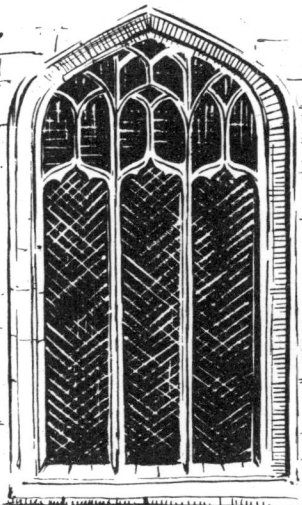

FINGLE BRIDGE. *See* DREWS-
TEIGNTON.

FRITHELSTOCK, on the Torridge, *c.* 11 miles SW. of Barnstaple,
with the ruins of an old Augustinian
priory near its interesting church
(carved bench-ends).

GEORGEHAM. A small resort
near the north coast, *c.* 8 miles NW.
of Barnstaple.

GEORGE NYMPTON, or NY-
MET (nim'et) **ST. GEORGE.** A
pretty place on the Mole, *c.* 12 miles
SE. of Barnstaple.

GERMANSWEEK, *c.* 25 miles N.
of Plymouth, is named from St.
German, to whom its church is
dedicated.

GIDLEIGH, on the edge of
Dartmoor, *c.* 16 miles W. of Exeter,
has, close by, the remains of the
fourteenth-century Gidleigh Castle
and numerous prehistoric formations,
including the Manor Pound, Scor-
hill and other circles, the 'Tolmen,'
or holed stone, and stone avenues on
Shovel Down.

GITTISHAM, *c.* 16 miles ENE. of
Exeter. The old mansion of Combe
was formerly residence of the Putt
family. There are some interesting
monuments in the church here.

GREAT TORRINGTON. *See*
TORRINGTON.

HACCOMBE, *c.* 5 miles NNW. of
Torquay. In the well-wooded grounds
of Haccombe House here is a chapel
with numerous memories of the
Carew family, including some excellent mediæval glass, monumental
brasses and effigies, and two horse-
shoes on the porch door. These last
support the local legend of a com-
petitive swim by a mounted Carew
and a Champernowne into Torbay,

Cottages in Lustleigh Village.

A holed Stone near Chagford.

the former winning the race and rescuing his distressed opponent.

HALBERTON. A pleasant village, *c.* 16 miles NNE. of Exeter. The ancient church of St. Andrew has a fine tenth-century screen and pulpit.

HARBERTON, *c.* 9 miles WSW. of Torquay. The fine Perpendicular church has an ancient stone screen and stone pulpit, and the almshouse dates from 1580.

HARFORD, on the Erme at the outskirts of Dartmoor, 10 miles ENE. of Plymouth. Close by are many hut circles and other prehistoric remains as well as signs of former tin-mining near the river.

HAWKCHURCH, *c.* 27 miles ENE. of Exeter. Wyld Court here, an Elizabethan mansion, was formerly the property of the Moore and Wyndham families.

HEMBURY FORT. *See* BROAD-HEMBURY.

HEMPSTONE, LITTLE, or **HEMPSTON ARUNDEL,** *c.* 6 miles WSW. of Torquay. The church has mediæval heraldic glass, originally belonging to Marldon church, and a fine rood screen. Old Manor here, a curious house dating from the thirteenth century, was formerly owned by the Arundels.

HEMYOCK, on the Culm, with excellent trout fishing, *c.* 20 miles NE. of Exeter. It has tennis courts and bowling greens.

HENNOCK, *c.* 9 miles SW. of Exeter, finely situated for views of Dartmoor to the west, of Torbay and Newton Abbott to the south, and of the Teign valley to the east. It has an ancient church.

HIGH WILLHAYS. *See* DART-MOOR.

HOLBETON, near the Erme mouth, *c.* 10 miles ESE of Plymouth, has screens of sixteenth-century wood carving in its church. Flete House is romantically situated on a height here and was originally seat of the Damerell family.

HOLCOMBE (hol'cum) **ROGUS,** *c.* 20 miles NE. of Exeter. Holcombe Court, said to be the finest Tudor mansion in Devon, includes a remarkable hall and gatehouse tower. The church contains numerous monuments to the Bluett family and parts of a rood screen from Tiverton church.

HORWOOD, *c.* 5 miles SW. of Barnstaple, has a church with interesting monuments to the Pollard family, an old pulpit, and some mediæval glass.

ILSINGTON, *c.* 13 miles SW. of Exeter, has a mediæval rood screen and carved bench ends in its church. On the moor here are many prehistoric remains.

INSTOW. A pleasure resort at the mouth of the Taw, 5 miles WSW. of Barnstaple. There are tennis courts here.

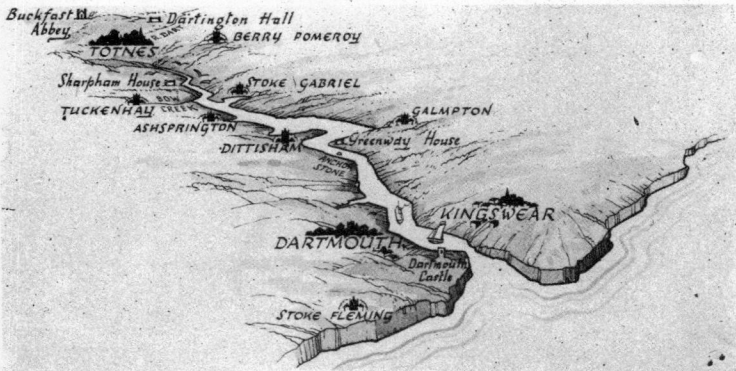

HOLNE (hōne), on the Dart, spanned here by the romantic Holne bridge, *c.* 15 miles WNW. of Torquay. Charles Kingsley was born in the vicarage here (1819) and there is a window to him in the old church (see also the ancient painted screen, pulpit, and mediæval glass). Hembury Camp, near-by, is a prehistoric fort, and there are numerous other barrows, hut circles and early camps in the district. Holne Chase, 'one of the finest examples of the ancient chase in the kingdom,' is close by.

There is trout fishing in the Dart.

IPPLEPEN, amid rocky scenery, *c.* 6 miles WNW. of Torquay. It has a painted rood screen and Jacobean pulpit in its church. In the centre of the village is an ancient wayside cross (now a Great War Memorial) Great Ambrook close by was originally a Norman manor. The Priory, a mansion surrounded by fine grounds, incorporates parts of what was anciently a priory here, attached to the Abbey of Fougères.

KELLY, *c.* 20 miles NNW. of Plymouth, with the manor house of the Kelly family, to whom there are monuments in the church, which should be visited also for its fragmentary mediæval glass.

KENN, *c.* 5 miles S. of Exeter, has a painted fifteenth-century screen in its church of St. Andrew, and an eight-hundred year old yew in its churchyard.

KENTISBEARE. A pretty village, *c.* 15 miles NE. of Exeter, with an ancient and excellent coloured wooden screen in its church.

KENTON, *c.* 7 miles SSE. of Exeter. Its church has a red sandstone tower, a large and richly-painted fifteenth-century rood screen, and an ancient pulpit.

KILMINGTON, *c.* 22 miles E. of Exeter. The Georgian mansion of Coryton Park stands in large, well-wooded grounds.

KINGSBRIDGE, at the head of Kingsbridge Creek, *c.* 20 miles ESE. of Plymouth. It has two ancient churches and a natural history museum. Near-by are the Shambles, a picturesque sixteenth-century arcade. There are bowling greens here and local trout fishing.

KINGSKERSWELL, *c.* 4 miles NW. of Torquay, has remains of an ancient castle and also an interesting church.

KING'S NYMPTON. *c.* 13 miles SE. of Barnstaple. The ancient church has a rich roof and screen. South-west of the village, in a well-wooded park, is the mansion of King's Nympton.

KINGSTEIGNTON (tayn'ton), *c.* 7 miles NW. of Torquay, noted for its pipe and potters' clay. In its church are some valuable 'chained' books.

Hackworthy Bridge near Walkhampton.

Holy Night! Silent Night!

A superstition prevailed in Devonshire that at midnight on Christmas Eve the oxen in their stalls were found on their knees in an attitude of devotion.

KINGSWEAR (kingz'weer), at the mouth of the Dart, opposite Dartmouth. Here is the ancient Kingswear Castle, and from the river bank a chain to Dartmouth Castle was extended to prevent the entrance of enemy ships.

KNOWSTONE, *c.* 20 miles NNW. of Exeter. Wadhams, now a farm house, was the seat of Sir Nicholas Wadham, founder of Wadham College, Oxford, in 1610.

LADRAM BAY. *See* SIDMOUTH.

LAMERTON, *c.* 17 miles N. of Plymouth. Collacombe Barton, now a farm house, is an Elizabethan mansion, former seat of the Tremaynes. It has a fine hall with a remarkable transomed window and sixteenth-century chimneypiece.

LEW, NORTH, *c.* 24 miles S. of Barnstaple. Its church has fine ancient bench ends, roofs of carved oak, and old embossed tiles in the tower.

LEW TRENCHARD. A pretty village, *c.* 20 miles N. of Plymouth. Lew House is interesting as the home of the late Rev. S. Baring-Gould, hymn writer (*Onward Christian Soldiers!*) and author of books on the south-west country. There is a 16-foot monolith at Lew Mill, close by.

LIFTON. A large village, *c.* 20 miles NNW. of Plymouth.

LITTLEHAM, 1. *c.* 10 miles SW. of Barnstaple. A wall painting of St. Swithin of the fourteenth century is to be seen in the church here.

2. A suburb of Exmouth.

LITTLE HEMPSTONE. *See* HEMPSTONE.

LODDISWELL. A village with excellent trout fishing facilities in the Avon valley, *c.* 18 miles SW. of Torquay. Close by are the remains of a British camp, 'The Rings.'

LOXHORE, on the Yeo, *c.* 6 miles NE. of Barnstaple, has curious fifteenth-century wooden pillars in its church.

LUFFINCOTT. A lovely place in the Tamar valley, *c.* 25 miles NNW. of Plymouth, with an allegedly haunted rectory.

PUFFIN

LUNDY ISLE ('island of puffins') A rock-bound island off the north coast, *c.* 12 miles NNW. of Hartland Point, the nesting place of myriads of sea-birds and former retreat of pirates, approachable from the east side only. A steamer service runs from Ilfracombe in the summer and a motor vessel from Barnstaple.

There are lighthouses, the ruins of the ancient Marisco Castle, and a chapel of St. Helen. It has an hotel.

MALBOROUGH, *c.* 20 miles SSE. of Plymouth, has a conspicuous church spire. Ilton Castle, a fourteenth-century fortified mansion, is now a farm house.

MAMHEAD, *c.* 7 miles S. of Exeter. In Mamhead Park is an obelisk (1743), a modern mansion in Elizabethan style, and some ancient trees.

MANATON, on the edge of

Ladram Bay

LUPPITT, on the Otter in pleasant surroundings, *c.* 20 miles ENE. of Exeter. The finely carved gateway of an ancient mansion of the Mohuns is to be seen close by.

LUSTLEIGH, on the fringes of Dartmoor, *c.* 10 miles SW. of Exeter, famous for its wooded gorge of Lustleigh Cleave. The church has ancient glass, a Tudor screen, and, in its porch, a Romano-British period stone. There is an old manor house here with a noble hall, and a logan stone lies near by.

LYMPSTONE. A pleasant village on the Exe estuary, *c.* 8 miles SSE. of Exeter.

Dartmoor, *c.* 15 miles SW. of Exeter, a good centre for visitors with antiquarian interests, on account of the prehistoric remains which abound on the surrounding tors and downs. (Kistvaens, logan stones, barrows and hut circles.)

MARLDON, *c.* 3 miles W. of Torquay. Compton Castle (fifteenth-century), partly ruined, has a gateway grooved for a portcullis, and an interesting chapel.

MARTINHOE. A picturesque coastal village with fine cliff scenery, *c.* 14 miles NE. of Barnstaple.

MARWOOD, *c.* 4 miles NNW. of

Old Trees at Manaton.

Barnstaple, has a fine screen dating from Henry VIII's time in its church.

MARYSTOW, or **MARY-STOWE**, *c.* 19 miles NNW. of Plymouth. Sydenham House, former seat of the Wise family (commemorated in the old church here) dates from the fourteenth century, but was altered and extended in the seventeenth century.

MARY TAVY (tay'vi), on the Tavy at the edge of Dartmoor, *c.* 16 miles N. of Plymouth. It has an ancient church and cross, and disused tin mine-workings may be seen in the valley close by.

MEAVY (mee'vi), *c.* 10 miles NNE. of Plymouth. Adjoining the church are the remains of a manor house once lived in by Sir Francis Drake, one of whose drums still summons the children to school here. There is an ancient cross under the Meavy oak.

MEMBURY, *c.* 24 miles ENE. of Exeter on the Yarty. Close by is Membury Castle Hill, a prehistoric camp, and Yarty, anciently seat of the Frys (see the monuments in Membury church), now a farm house.

MILTON ABBOT, *c.* 17 miles NNW. of Plymouth. Endsleigh, a picturesque 'Swiss' building (1810), residence of the Duke of Bedford, is surrounded by beautiful grounds traversed by the Tamar.

MOLLAND, *c.* 17 miles ESE. of Barnstaple. There are disused copper and manganese mines close by. Great Champson, now a farm house, formerly residence of the Chulm and Champeaux families, has excellent old panelling and screens, while West

Bull Point Lighthouse, Mortehoe.

Clapper Bridge at Postbridge.   Arcades in Plympton St. Mary.

Molland was the residence of the Courtenays.

MONKLEIGH, *c.* 10 miles SW. of Barnstaple. Annery House has a well-wooded park. Little of the ancient house remains, however. There is an Annery aisle in the church, which has ancient carved bench ends.

MORTEHOE, or **MORTE.** A coastal village, *c.* 11 miles NW. of Barnstaple. On Morte Pound is Bull Point Lighthouse and a fog-horn, and a fixed warning light on the Morte Stone, a dangerous shoal off the point. There is an ancient church in Mortehoe.

MUSBURY, *c.* 22 miles E. of Exeter. Ashe House here was the seat of the Drakes, to whom there are numerous monuments in Musbury church. The Duke of Marlborough, son of Elizabeth Drake, was born here in 1650. A hill-top earthwork can be seen near by.

NEWTON FERRERS, at the Yealm mouth, *c.* 8 miles SE. of Plymouth.

NORTH BOVEY. *See* BOVEY.

NORTHLEIGH, *c.* 18 miles E. of Exeter, has some mediæval glass in its interesting old church.

NORTH LEW. *See* LEW.

NORTH MOLTON. *See* MOLTON.

NORTH TAWTON. *See* TAWTON.

OGWELL, EAST and **WEST.** Two adjacent villages, some 8 miles NW. of Torquay, both having interesting ancient churches. West Ogwell House, former seat of the Reynells, stands in pleasant grounds.

OTTERTON, on the Otter, near the south coast, *c.* 12 miles SE. of Exeter, near the beautiful Ladram Bay to the east, ancient seat of a Benedictine Priory attached to Mont St. Michel in France.

PARRACOMBE, *c.* 12 miles NE. of Barnstaple, has an interesting ancient church. There are prehistoric remains, including Chapman Barrows, near-by. What is left of Holwell Castle dates from the tenth century.

PAYHEMBURY, *c.* 14 miles ENE. of Exeter, has an ancient painted screen in its church.

PETER TAVY (tay'vi), finely situated at the edge of Dartmoor, *c.* 16 miles N. of Plymouth, within easy access of the numerous prehistoric remains on the slopes of Cox, Roos and White Tors. It has an interesting church.

PINHOE. A suburb of Exeter.

PLYMPTON EARLE, *c.* 6 miles E. of Plymouth, till 1832 a borough returning two members to Parliament.

PLYMPTON ST. MARY, *c.* 4 miles ENE. of Plymouth. Saltram House, seat of the Earl of Morley, stands in a wooded park overlooking the Laira (estuary of the Plym), and contains valuable paintings by Reynolds. There is a Perpendicular church of St. Mary and remains of a twelfth-century Cistercian priory. Bonington House, now a farm house, contains a fine hall and minstrels' gallery. Other notable mansions here are Old Newnham and Newnham Park. Plympton St. Mary well repays a visit.

PLYMSTOCK, *c.* 3 miles SE. of Plymouth, has monuments to the

Harris family in its fine fifteenth-century church.

PLYMTREE, c. 13 miles NE. of Exeter, has in its church a magnificent screen with portraits of Henry VII, his son Arthur, and Cardinal Morton, in the guise of the three Magi. It has fine panelling and bench ends.

POOL, SOUTH. A picturesquely situated village in a deep valley, on an arm of Salcombe estuary, c. 18 miles SW. of Torquay.

PORTLEMOUTH. A coastal village, c. 20 miles SW. of Torquay, standing on a height on the east side of Salcombe estuary. The rood screen of its church has ancient painted figures of saints. Portlemouth is connected to Salcombe by ferry.

POSTBRIDGE, in the middle of Dartmoor, c. 17 miles WSW. of Exeter, on the East Dart, spanned here by an old clapper bridge, an excellent centre for examination of the very numerous prehistoric antiquities close by (stone rows, kistvaens and hut circles).

There is trout fishing in the neighbourhood.

POWDERHAM, c. 6 miles SSE. of Exeter. Powderham Castle, in fine grounds, a residence of the Earls of Devon, was originally built in the thirteenth century. Lawrence Castle, or the Belvedere (60 feet), on a wooded hill, stands on the site of an ancient British camp.

There is local trout fishing here.

RATTERY, c. 12 miles WSW. of Torquay. There is a Bridgettine nunnery here which has had a continuous existence since 1415.

RINGMORE. A pleasant coastal village, c. 13 miles ESE. of Plymouth, with bold cliff scenery. The ancient Journey's End Inn (licensed) close by should be visited. There is an 18-hole golf course at Bigbury-on-Sea.

ROCKBEARE, c. 7 miles ENE. of Exeter. Part of Rockbeare Hill here has been National Trust property since 1904.

ROSE ASH, c. 16 miles ESE. of Barnstaple. A clock in the church tower commemorates an unbroken succession (250 years) of eight rectors of the Southcomb family.

ST. MARYCHURCH. See Torquay.

SAMPFORD COURTENAY, c. 16 miles WNW. of Exeter, was scene of the initial rising in the Prayer Book rebellion, and has an interesting church.

SAMPFORD PEVERELL, c. 15 miles NNE. of Exeter, ancient seat of the Peverells, who had a castle here.

SANDFORD, on the Creedy, c. 10 miles NW. of Exeter. Creedy Park here, a modern house in the Tudor style, stands in extensive well-wooded grounds. Part of the old building remains. Other mansions close by are Bremridge, Ruxford Barton and Coombe Lancelles.

SHALDON. See Teignmouth.

SHAUGH (shaw) **PRIOR,** on the edge of Dartmoor, c. 7 miles NE. of Plymouth, near the junction of the Plym and the Meavy. There are numerous ancient crosses and prehistoric remains on the moor here, a fine old font cover in the church, and local china clay works.

SHEEPSTOR. A charming vill-

Facing: Old Manor at Shute.

age on the fringes of Dartmoor, *c.* 10 miles NNE. of Plymouth (which is supplied with water from Burraton Reservoir here). Near-by is an ancient ('Pixies') cave on Sheepstor, which overlooks, and gives name to, the village.

SHERFORD, *c.* 17 miles SSW. of Torquay, has a rich screen in its church and an interesting old pulpit. Keynedon, a farm house, is Tudor, and former residence of the Hals family.

SHERWELL, or **SHIRWELL**. A pleasant village, *c.* 4 miles NE. of Barnstaple.

SHUTE, *c.* 20 miles E. of Exeter, with monuments in its church to the Pole family, whose arms are upon an ancient gateway of Shute mansion near-by.

SIDBURY, on the Sid, *c.* 14 miles E. of Exeter, with interesting Saxon and Norman features in its church. Sand, now a farm house, was the seat of the Huish family. The modern Sidbury Manor stands in an extensive deer park. Sidbury Castle, to the west, is a Roman camp.

SLAPTON, on the coast, *c.* 14 miles SSW. of Torquay, has fragmentary mediæval glass in its church and near it the gateway of what was anciently a monastic college. Poole, now a farm house, was the ancient residence of the Hawkins. There is good coarse fishing and shooting on the Lea, a lagoon-like lake close by.

SOURTON, *c.* 23 miles W. of Exeter, on the edge of Dartmoor.

SOUTH BRENT. *See* BRENT.

SOUTH MOLTON. *See* MOLTON.

SOUTH POOL. *See* POOL.

SOUTH SYDENHAM. *See* SYDENHAM DAMEREL.

SOUTH TAWTON. *See* TAWTON.

SPREYTON, *c.* 15 miles WNW. of Exeter, with a fifteenth-century timber roof in its church.

STAVERTON, on the Dart, here spanned by an ancient seven-arched bridge, *c.* 7 miles W. of Torquay. The church of St. Paul de Lyon here has a fine rood screen. Many of the houses are roofed with green and reddish slate from local quarries. There is a limestone cavern at Pridhamsleigh, an old house, near-by.

Trout fishing is available in the river.

STICKLEPATH, *c.* 16 miles W. of Exeter, has an old well and, near it, an ancient inscribed stone.

STOCKLEIGH. Two pleasant villages with ancient churches.

1. **Stockleigh English** (from its 'English' owner after the Conquest), *c.* 10 miles NW. of Exeter.

2. **Stockleigh Pomeroy** (from its owner at the time of the Conquest), *c.* 8 miles NNW. of Exeter.

STOKE FLEMING, on the precipitous coast, *c.* 10 miles SSW. of Torquay, has a fine fourteenth-century brass in its church. Close by is Blackpool, a good bathing cove.

STOKE GABRIEL, on a branch of the Dart estuary, *c.* 6 miles SW. of Torquay. Its church has an ancient pulpit, a black letter and a 'vinegar' bible. Davis, the navigator, whose name is borne by the Straits which he discovered in 1585, was a native. Some distance to the south-east are the mansions of Sandridge Park and Waddeton Court.

Fresh Water Fishing in Devonshire

DEVONSHIRE has been described by one authority as the most troutful county in the south of England. It has certainly many more streams than the average—all of them trout-containing and flowing for the most part through the pleasantest of scenery. Licences are usually obtainable locally, or, if not, they may be had through the Board of Conservators of Fishery Districts in Exeter.

AVON. A stream rising in Dartmoor which offers small trout.
Flies (brown trout):
 March Brown Spring.
 Blue Dun
 Cochybonddhu

 Black Gnat Summer and
 Blue Dun autumn.
 Red Palmer

AXE. A fine clear river with salmon and trout in it.
Flies (brown trout):
 March Brown.
 Red Palmer.
 Blue Dun.

CREEDY. A tributary of the Exe yielding good brown trout.
Flies (brown trout):
 March Brown.
 Red Palmer.
 Blue Upright.

CULM. A pleasant little stream offering quite good brown trout, especially in the spring months.

Flies (brown trout)
 March Brown.
 Blue Dun.
 May Fly

DART. This notable water rises in Dartmoor, and flows through magnificent scenery. It has a clear and swift current.
Flies (brown trout):
 Red Palmer.
 March Brown.
 Silver Blue.

ERME. A river rising in Dartmoor affording good sea trout fishing in the spring and early summer, and brown trout in its upper reaches. The sea trout are mostly taken on bait.
Flies (brown trout):
 Red Palmer.
 March Brown.
 Blue Dun.

EXE. A beautiful trout and salmon river with a course of over 60 miles. It is normally clear, but becomes reddish in flood.

Flies (brown trout):
- March Brown.
- Blue Upright.
- Grannom.
- Blue Dun.
- Olive Dun.

OKEMENT. A moorland stream where fish are numerous but small.
Flies (brown trout):
- Blue Upright.
- Olive Dun.
- March Brown.

OTTER. Once a capital brown-trout stream, now much depleted.
Flies (brown trout):
- Blue Upright.
- Partridge Quill.
- Yellow Dun.

TAMAR. This river on much of its course separates Devonshire and Cornwall. Brown trout, sea trout, and occasionally rainbow trout are caught.
Flies (brown trout):
- Cochybonddhu.
- Blue Dun.
- March Brown.
- Alexandra.

TAW. A north-flowing river, rising in Dartmoor, offering an occasional salmon in its lower reaches. The minnow is chiefly used for trout.
Flies (brown trout):
- Red Palmer.
- Silver Palmer.
- Olive Dun.
- March Brown.

TEIGN. A fine stream which, at several times in the past, has been seriously polluted. This has been efficiently dealt with by the fishing associations on the river, which now offers some salmon, brown trout, and a run of sea trout in the spring and early autumn.
Flies (brown trout):
- March Brown.
- Blue Dun.
- Silver Blue.

Flies (sea trout):
- Red Palmer.
- Blue and Silver.
- Alexandra.

TORRIDGE. A rapid river running to the sea at Bideford, forming a long estuary with the Taw. It offers some salmon, sea trout and brown trout. The first and second are to be taken chiefly on the minnow.
Flies (brown trout):
- March Brown.
- Red Palmer.
- Blue Dun.

WALKHAM. A Dartmoor brook with a rocky, wooded course, best fished for trout in the spring months.
Flies (brown trout):
- Blue Dun.
- Cochybonddhu.
- Red Spinner.

YEALM. A thickly wooded stream yielding small trout.
Flies (brown trout):
- Cochybonddhu.
- Blue Upright.
- Red Palmer.

STOKE–IN–TEIGNHEAD (tin′ hed), *c.* 5 miles N. of Torquay, has a fine early brass, dated 1375, and a good screen in its church.

STOKENHAM, *c.* 15 miles SSW. of Torquay, land-marked by its fine church tower. There is good coarse fishing to be had in 'the Lea' close by.

STONEHOUSE. *See* PLYMOUTH.

STOWFORD. A pleasantly situated village, on a tributary of the Lyd, *c.* 20 miles N. of Plymouth. Hayne house was formerly the seat of the Mohun Harris family to whom there are monuments in the church.

SUTCOMBE, *c.* 20 miles SW. of Barnstaple. Its church has ancient wood carving in the fine rood screen, pulpit and bench ends, as well as mediæval glass and old tiles.

SWIMBRIDGE, or **SWYM-BRIDGE**, *c.* 4 miles SE. of Barnstaple, has a fine Perpendicular church with a magnificent oak rood screen. Jack Russell, 'the sporting parson,' was vicar here from 1832 to 1880.

SYDENHAM DAMEREL, or **SOUTH SYDENHAM**. A village in magnificent scenery, near the Tamar, 14 miles NNW. of Plymouth.

TAMAR. A river, forming in part of its course the boundary between Devon and Cornwall, enters the sea by Plymouth Sound. The Tavy and the Plym are its chief affluents, and these and the Tamar provide good trout fishing.

TAW. A river, rising in Dartmoor and flowing north through Barnstaple to join the estuary of the Torridge.

TAWSTOCK, *c.* 2 miles S. of Barnstaple. A gateway alone remains of the original Tawstock Court here, seat of the Bourchier Wrey family. The present building stands in a well-wooded park. There is some mediæval glass, an old pulpit, bench ends and good monuments to the Bourchier family in the church.

TAWTON. 1. **North Tawton**. A pleasant market town, *c.* 18 miles WNW. of Exeter.

2. **South Tawton**. A village, *c.* 17 miles W. of Exeter.

Oxenham Manor house, 1 mile to the east, was seat of the family of that name (*see* Kingley's *Westward Ho!*)

TEIGN (tĭn). A river rising in Dartmoor and flowing to the sea at Teignmouth. It has a long, narrow estuary, and affords trout fishing.

TEIGNGRACE, or **TEIGN-RACE**, on the Teign at the head of the Stover canal, *c.* 8 miles NW. of Torquay. The pleasant classical Stover house here, now a girls' school, stands in a well-wooded park.

TETCOTT, near the Tamar, *c.* 28 miles NNW. of Plymouth, well known for its foxhounds and hunts. The partly demolished Tetcott House, with its grounds, was reputedly haunted by the Arscotts of Tetcott, to whom there are monuments in the church.

THORVERTON. A village, *c.* 7 miles N. of Exeter. Trout fishing in the Exe is available.

THURLESTONE (thurl′ston: 'pierced rock' — from Thurlstone Rock, a natural arch on the coast here), near the south coast, *c.* 16 miles ESE. of Plymouth. There are tennis courts, riding facilities, and an 18-hole golf course.

TORBRIAN, *c.* 7 miles WNW. of Torquay, has magnificent ancient woodwork in its pulpit, pews, and screens (painted) and mediæval glass, notably in the east window. Tor Newton House here was formerly the seat of the Petre family.

TORRIDGE. A good trout-fishing stream rising near Clovelly and entering the sea by a wide estuary below Bideford. Its chief tributary is the Okement, and the Taw flows into its estuary.

TRENTISHOE, near the north coast, *c.* 12 miles NE. of Barnstaple. Close by is Heddon's Mouth, a renowned rocky valley, and there is magnificent woodland and cliff scenery in the neighbourhood.

TRUSHAM. A village near the Teign, 8 miles SW. of Exeter, with an interesting ancient church.

UFFCULME (uf'cum), on the Culm, *c.* 16 miles NE. of Exeter, has a richly carved, ancient rood screen and monuments to the **Walrond** family in its church. The sixteenth-century mansion of Bradfield stands in extensive grounds here.

Trout fishing is obtainable in the Culm.

UGBOROUGH, *c.* 12 miles E. of Plymouth, on the southern edge of Dartmoor, rich in tumuli, stone rows, old crosses and other prehistoric remains here, overlooked by Ugborough Beacon (1,231 feet). Ugborough church has part of a magnificent fifteenth-century screen, with traces of Jacobean painting upon it, a Norman font, and an ancient pulpit.

UPTON PYNE, *c.* 4 miles N. of Exeter, has a fine conspicuous tower on its ancient red sandstone church. Pynes, originally designed by Inigo Jones, stands on a height in a large well-wooded park here.

WALKHAMPTON, on the edge of Dartmoor, *c.* 10 miles NNE. of Plymouth. It has a sixteenth-century church house with an ancient oak roof.

The DEVIL in WIDECOMBE

On the evening of 21st October, 1638, a rider, mounted on a jet-black horse, entered the Poundstock Inn, asked his way to Widecombe, and ordered a glass of ale.

The landlord's wife, who drew the ale, observed that it hissed and bubbled as it went down the black rider's gullet. She shrieked, and the Devil, for it was no less, careered off, dashed into Widecombe Church, seized an unfortunate boy asleep during the service, and disappeared with him through the roof.

Blackpool Sands near Stoke Fleming.

WASHFIELD, *c.* 16 miles N. of Exeter. The church of St. Mary the Virgin has a fine Jacobean screen and interesting brasses and monuments.

WEARE GIFFORD (weer ji'ford), or **WEAR GIFFORD**, *c.* 9 miles SW. of Barnstaple. Weare Hall here has a fine panelled hall, with hammer beam roof, as well as an ancient tower and gateway. The famous Fortescue family is commemorated in monuments and ancient glass in Weare Gifford Church.

WELCOMBE, amid wild scenery on the north coast, *c.* 22 miles WSW. of Barnstaple, with an early carved oak screen, and other interesting woodwork in its church.

WEMBURY. An attractive coastal village, 6 miles SE. of Plymouth.

WEMBWORTHY, *c.* 16 miles SSE. of Barnstaple. The Elizabethan Rashleigh mansion close by is now a farm house.

WERRINGTON, on the Tamar, *c.* 20 miles NNW. of Plymouth. The Georgian Werrington Hall here stands in extensive well-wooded grounds.

WEST . ALVINGTON. *See* ALVINGTON.

WEST DOWN. *See* DOWN.

WEST OGWELL. *See* OGWELL.

WEST WORLINGTON. *See* WORLINGTON.

WHIMPLE. A pleasant village, *c.* 9 miles ENE. of Exeter.

WHITCHURCH, *c.* 12 miles N. of Plymouth. Close to Whitchurch is the 18-hole Tavistock golf course. To the NE. is Holwell, an ancient mansion standing in well-wooded grounds.

WHITESTONE. A village, *c.* 3 miles NW. of Exeter.

WIDECOMBE–IN–THE–MOOR (wid'di-cum). A pleasant moorland village, *c.* 19 miles SW. of Exeter. Its church has a magnificent tower, and was possibly endowed by the once prosperous tin miners here. The fair, which gave name to the celebrated song, is held in September.

WIDWORTHY, *c.* 18 miles ENE. of Exeter. Widworthy Court here,

---

ROYAL · OAK DAY, 29ᵗʰ May

To commemorate the marvellous escape of Charles II in 1651, after his defeat by Cromwell.

At Tiverton a procession of young men dressed in seventeenth-century style paraded the streets, their leader called Oliver, dressed in black, with hands and face covered with grease and soot, held captive by a stout rope. This grim figure capered and leapt in ridiculous fashion to the great amusement of the spectators and awe of the children. Another band followed bearing emblematic branches of oak.

property of the Marwood family, is a nineteenth-century mansion in fine grounds.

WILLAND, *c.* 16 miles NE. of Exeter, has a good ancient screen with traces of colour and gilding in its church.

WISTMAN'S WOOD. *See* DARTMOOR.

WOODBURY, *c.* 7 miles SE. of Exeter, overlooked on the E. by 'Woodbury Castle,' the remains of a British and Roman encampment.

WOOLACOMBE, *c.* 10 miles NW. of Barnstaple, has well-known sands.

WORLINGTON, EAST and **WEST.** Two pretty villages, *c.* 15 miles NW. of Exeter. **West Worling-ton** has an old church with a wooden spire. Close by is Affeton Castle, an embattled gateway of the old building alone remaining.

YEALM, rises in Dartmoor and flows south to enter the sea by Yealm Mouth, a long estuary.

YEALMPTON (yam'ton), on the Yealm, near the head of its estuary, *c.* 7 miles ESE. of Plymouth.

YELVERTON, *c.* 10 miles NNE. of Plymouth. A good walking centre for western Dartmoor, it has an 18-hole golf course, bowling greens and local trout fishing.

YES TOR. *See* DARTMOOR.

ZEAL MONACHORUM ('monastic cell'—once attached to the Abbey of Buckfastleigh). A village, *c.* 14 miles WNW. of Exeter.

A Scene in Widecombe.

CORNWALL

CORNISH ROADS

The fairy roads of Cornwall don't lead you anywhere at all,
And if you try to travel them, to riddle or unravel them,
You'll find you're in a prickle bush or up against a wall.

For the merry men of Cornwall that used to trade in tin,
That never used to hurry 'em, to bother or to worry 'em,
That never liked a job of work—they took the fairies in.

And when the men of Cornwall wanted tin, or milk, or grain,
The fairies used to send a band of workers for to lend a hand,
Who, when they'd done a good day's work, would hurry home
    again.

But when the winds in winter batter'd down the stunted trees,
They would scamper helter-skelter to the Cornishman for
    shelter,
And share his fire, and drink his beer, and eat his bread and
    cheese.

But some giants came to Cornwall with level, pole, and chain,
And put up signposts all around, and drew broad arrows on the
    ground,
And tried to tar the twisting road and straighten out the lane.

Then the fairy folk of Cornwall said they'd know the reason why!
They seized the posts and shattered them, and tore them up and
    scattered them,
And took away the arrows, or turned them all awry.

So don't ever go to Cornwall and try to find the way
From Goonbell into Trabulo, or on to Perranzabuloe,
From Indian Queens to Summercourt or Mevagissey Bay.

For the roads that run in Cornwall are merry roads to tread;
They do not seem to mind about however much they wind about,
And if you think they'll take you there they'll bring you back
    instead.

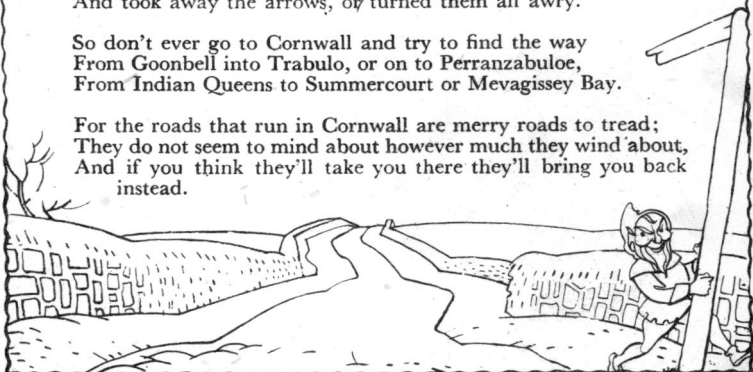

93

Facing: *A Cornish Ford on Bodmin Moor.*

Boscastle Harbour.
Bodmin : The Hermit's Cell.

ST. AGNES. A small mining town near the north coast, overlooked by the Beacon (600 feet), *c.* 8 miles WNW. of Truro.

Harmony Cot, close by, was the birthplace of Opie the painter. Near St. Agnes is Travaunance Cove, where good bathing and tennis are available.

ST. AGNES (Scilly). *See* SCILLY ISLES.

ST. AUSTELL. A town and resort, centre of the Cornish china clay industry, *c.* 14 miles ENE. of Truro.

St. Austell is built on a hilly site near St. Austell Bay on the south coast, and safe bathing is obtainable in the numerous sandy coves in the vicinity. Bowling greens, tennis courts, and four cinemas are available to visitors.

The church has a fine granite tower and contains some ancient stained glass.

BODMIN

BODMIN ('abode of the monks'), the county town of Cornwall, lies *c.* 22 miles SW. of Launceston. Bodmin is an excellent starting point for walks in the district, and the town has bowling greens, tennis courts and cinemas.

The large church of St. Petrock is chiefly in the Perpendicular style, and has the remains of a priory chapel near it, and two ancient wells. There is a good town hall and a free library.

Numerous earthworks and ancient crosses are to be seen in the neighbourhood. In the desolate Bodmin Moors to the east lies Dozmary Pool, the largest lake in Cornwall, held by some to have witnessed the loss of Arthur's sword 'Excalibur.'

About 4 miles NW. is Pencarrow, Elizabethan seat of the Molesworths, one of the finest mansions in the county. In its surroundings are two ancient camps.

BOSCASTLE (or **FORRA-BURY**). A small coastal town, on a wild, romantic site, with a fascinating little harbour, *c.* 17 miles NNE. of Bodmin. On a headland is the church of Forrabury. Trout fishing is available in the stream here, and there are tennis courts and a bathing pool.

BUDE, or BUDE HAVEN. A popular seaport and holiday resort on Bude Bay, *c.* 15 miles NNW. of Launceston. There are fine sands and cliff scenery, and Bude is admirably placed for visiting such attractions as Tintagel, Boscastle, Hartland and Clovelly.

There is an excellent 18-hole golf course (Bude and North Cornwall Club), a 9-hole course on Summerleaze Downs, tennis courts, bowling greens, and a cinema. Good bathing is available on the sands below Summerleaze and Maer Downs, and there is a bathing pool in the rocks close by. Anglers may obtain trout fishing in the reservoirs.

CALLINGTON. Formerly a prosperous mining town, *c.* 10 miles S. of Launceston.

St. Mary's Church is an interesting Perpendicular granite building. Within the structure the figures of monks carved on the soles of the effigy of Lord Willoughby de Broke are almost unique. 5 miles E. is Cotehele, ancestral home of the Edgcumbes There is a very complete holy well about 1 mile to the south-east of Callington.

On Hingston Down, to the north-east, the Saxons under Edgar defeated a combined Cornish and Danish army in 835, with much bloodshed.

There is a cinema here.

CAMBORNE. A market town *c.* 10 miles WNW. of Falmouth. There are bowling greens, tennis courts, and a golf course here. Richard Trevethick, inventor of the high-pressure steam engine, was a native.

CAMELFORD (Tennyson's *Camelot*). An ancient town and a resort of growing importance, on the Camel, 12 miles N. of Bodmin.

There is trout fishing in the river and other streams here, golf at Tintagel, and bathing on the sands

Tintagel.

Falmouth Harbour—a copper engraving.

96

at Trebarwith, *c.* 4 miles NNW. of the town. Camelford is an excellent 'jumping-off' place for Tintagel, Dozmary Pool, Brown Willy, and the many prehistoric remains that are scattered on the moor to the S.

CHARLESTOWN. A seaport, *c.* 12 miles S. of Bodmin, named from Charles Rashleigh, who constructed the harbour here. Good sea fishing is available locally and Charlestown has a swimming pool and tennis courts.

ST. COLUMB MAJOR, *c.* 12 miles WSW. of Bodmin, has a fine church and, near-by, prehistoric remains (Castle-an-Dinas, a headland camp, and the Nine Maidens, a stone row). There is a cinema here.

St. Columb Minor is a village near Newquay.

ST. DAY. A small town, *c.* 6 miles NNW. of Falmouth.

FALMOUTH

A BOROUGH, seaport and popular resort on the south coast, on the Fal estuary, overlooking the wide sea-inlet of Carrick Roads. It has a magnificent harbour dominated by Pendennis and St. Mawes castles.

Open spaces in Falmouth include Kimberley Park, Queen Mary and Gyllyngdune and Rosehill Gardens. Good sea-bathing on Gyllyngvase, Swanpool and Castle Beaches, and sailing is available.

Other attractions for visitors include tennis courts, bowling greens, three cinemas, dance halls and a summer pavilion with resident concert party, sea-fishing and steamer trips.

The church was dedicated to King Charles the Martyr in 1663. The ancient church of St. Budock lies 2 miles to the west.

Falmouth was the port of departure of the famous 'packet' boats.

Penjerrich estate, 3 miles to the south-west, has associations with the Foxes of Quaker fame.

The Coast at Bude.

Tintagel : King Arthur's Castle.

FOWEY (foy). A borough since Elizabethan times, market town and port on Fowey river and harbour, 12 miles SSE. of Bodmin.

There is a 9-hole golf course and a yacht club here, a regatta being held in August. In addition Fowey offers the visitor tennis courts, bowling and putting greens, excellent seafishing, and a cinema.

A chain for the protection of the harbour used to run between Fowey and Polruan on the east side of the river, where there are ruins of a chapel and holy well.

The town furnished Edward III with forty-seven ships for the Siege of Calais in 1346, and the French landed here and burnt the town in 1457. Its seamen bore the proud title of the Fowey 'gallaunts.' Sir Arthur Quiller-Couch had close associations with this place.

Fowey is a loading harbour for china clay.

In the town is Place, seat of the Treffrys, a mansion originally built in the eleventh century. It contains Tudor panelling and heraldry.

The Fowey river rises in the Bodmin Moors, and flows through Lostwithiel to its estuary on the south coast here.

ST. GERMANS, *c.* 17 miles S. of Launceston. There are vestiges of a Celtic church here dedicated to St. Germans, and also of Athelstan's Saxon building. The Norman church which succeeded these was part of an Augustinian Priory and forms the greater part of the present structure, which also contains features of later date.

A cattle fair is held here in May. Port Eliot, a large mansion, is the seat of the Earl of St. Germans.

GRAMPOUND. A former borough, on the Fal, *c.* 8 miles ENE. of Truro. There are extensive remains of prehistoric camps in the neighbourhood. Bowling greens and tennis courts are available for visitors.

HAYLE. A town on St. Ives Bay at the estuary of the Hayle, *c.* 8 miles NE. of Penzance, the traditional landing-place in early times of the Irish saints.

There is a cinema here.

HELSTON ('fortress on the marsh') A borough, market town and resort of growing importance on the Cober, *c.* 12 miles WSW. of Falmouth.

On the 8th of May, by ancient custom Helston holds a festival (the 'Furry'), and is gaily bedecked with flowers, while a celebrated dance is performed by children and adults through the streets to a musical accompaniment.

The public park here has tennis courts, putting course and bowling greens and the town has a cinema.

To the south-west is Penrose, anciently seat of the family of that name, since 1770 of the Rogers family.

To the south of Helston, Loe Pool, a lake formed by the Cober, is alleged by some to have been the scene of the loss of Arthur's sword 'Excalibur' (*see* also Bodmin).

HOLSWORTHY. A small town, *c.* 24 miles SW. of Barnstaple, a hunting centre and scene, in July, of the ancient St. Peter's Fair. There are tennis courts here and local trout fishing.

✗ Some Cornish Golf Courses

								Day	Week
BUDE	.	.	.	.	.	.	.	5/–	25/–
CAMBORNE	.	.	.	.	.	.	.	5/–	21/–
ST. ENODOC (Wadebridge)	.	.	.	.	.	.	5/–	25/–
FOWEY	.	.	.	.	.	.	.	2/–	10/–
LELANT	.	.	.	.	.	.	(1)	5/–	21/–
							(2)	3/6	15/–
MULLION	.	.	.	.	.	.	.	5/–	20/–
NEWQUAY	.	.	.	.	.	.	.	6/–	27/6
PERRANPORTH	.	.	.	.	.	.	.	5/–	20/–
TINTAGEL	.	.	.	.	.	.	.	3/–	10/6
TREVOSE (Padstow)	.	.	.	.	.	.	5/–	25/–
WHITSAND BAY (Torpoint)	.	.	.	.	.	.	4/6	21/–

St. Ives : The Harbour and the Beach.

ST. IVES

ST. IVES (from St. Ia, who landed here in the fifth century). A borough, fishing town and popular holiday resort on St. Ives Bay, 7 miles NNE. of Penzance.

Excellent bathing is available at Porthminster and Porthmeor Beaches, and there are facilities for sailing, sea-fishing, tennis and bowling. There is an 18-hole golf course at Lelant (West Cornwall Golf Club), 4 miles to the south-east. Hotels and boarding-houses, shops and cafés are to be found in profusion. The Municipal Concert Hall is one of the finest in the West.

The old part of the town has winding streets and ancient houses, and there is an interesting harbour. The church dates from the fifteenth century. Near its south door is a cross of similar date.

St. Ives was formerly outstanding for its seine net pilchard fisheries.

To the south-west is Carbis Bay with its magnificent sands, a holiday haunt of growing importance.

ST.-JUST-IN-PENWITH (named possibly from a Welsh saint). A town near the north coast, *c.* 7 miles WNW. of Penzance. The church is mostly of fifteenth century.

There is a cinema here.

LAUNCESTON. The former county town of Cornwall, situated on a hill near the Devon border.

Launceston Castle, of which practically all that remains is the keep, overlooks the town and commands magnificent views of the surrounding country. Near-by is Launceston Priory, the remains of an ancient Augustinian foundation. A Norman doorway removed from this may be seen at the White Hart Hotel.

St. Mary Magdalene's church, built by Sir Henry Trecarel, dates in large part from the fifteenth century, its exterior having much elaborate ornament in carved granite, and its interior interesting ancient woodwork and monuments.

The old south gate to the town still stands, and above it is a museum. Portions of the town walls remain.

There are cinemas, swimming baths, tennis courts, bowling greens and a public library.

The noble Norman doorway of the White Hart Hotel in Launceston, originally part of Launceston Priory. Notice the elaborate carving on the rounded arch. The detail has wonderfully survived eight centuries of weathering

Above : Trevethy Quoit.

Below : A Cave near Mullion.

Facing : Land's End : Dr. Syntax's Head.

Looe Harbour.

LISKEARD. A borough and market town on the Looe, *c.* 14 miles SSW. of Launceston. Large cattle fairs are held here monthly, and there is an annual fair in October.

The church of St. Martin is one of the largest in Cornwall. It has an Early English tower, a Jacobean pulpit and an ancient lych-gate. Round Liskeard a number of holy wells are to be found. The town has a public library and bowling green.

THE LIZARD. A name extended in application to cover the whole peninsular area to the south-east of Helston, containing Lizard Point and the little town of Lizard. The headland has two light-houses.

LOOE. A small town of great antiquity, picturesquely situated on Looe Bay, on the south coast, at the mouth of the Looe, *c.* 15 miles SE. of Bodmin.

Sea-bathing, excellent fishing and boating are to be had here, river trips in the tidal creeks and sea cruises along the coast are arranged daily. There are two cinemas.

Looe really consists of East and West Looe on the east and west bank of the river respectively, connected by a fine stone bridge. Its most notable building is the old Guild Hall and pillory. Off the coast lies Looe Island.

The town contributed over twenty ships to the Siege of Calais in 1346.

LOSTWITHIEL. A borough and market town on the Fowey, here crossed by a fourteenth-century bridge, *c.* 6 miles SSE. of Bodmin. There is good trout fishing to be had here, and some magnificent scenery in the surrounding district. Lanhydrock and Boconnoc, with their fine grounds, are within easy walking distance. Lostwithiel has bowling greens and a cinema.

This was at one time the sole coinage town of Cornwall, and there are traces of an old stannary court to be seen at Duchy House. St. Bartholomew's Church has a fine lantern spire. The ruins of Restormel Castle lie about 1 mile to the north.

MARAZION, or MARKET JEW, *c.* 4 miles E. of Penzance, in a sheltered position, enjoying an exceptionally mild climate, said by some to have been the scene of the Phœnicians' tin trading (from which its name, meaning 'market,' may de-

rive). There is a fair in September.

St. Michael's Mount (230 feet), off the coast here in Mounts Bay, connected at low water with Marazion by a causeway, has a castle on the site of an ancient priory, and, near it, an interesting old chapel. The Mount bears a striking resemblance to Mont St. Michel off the French coast, and

Cornish Pasties

½ lb. short-crust pastry
Finely-cut raw beef
Dried raw potato
Some chopped onion
Mixed herbs

Mix vegetables together with meat, herbs and seasoning. Add a little stock or gravy. Cut rounds of pastry and place a little of the mixture upon each. Moisten the edges and press together. Glaze with egg or milk. Bake for 1 hour.

St. Michael's Mount—from an old print.

The Beach at Newquay.

was in fact granted to the Abbey of St. Michel by Edward the Confessor.

To the east of Mounts Bay are Prussia Cove, so-called from its being the resort of an eighteenth-century smuggler, John Carter, who styled himself 'King of Prussia,' the fine Praa Sands, and the remains of Pengersick Castle.

MEVAGISSEY. A popular resort for anglers and artists, c. 6 miles S. of St. Austell on Mevagissey Bay. It is celebrated for its pilchard fisheries.

NEWLYN. A celebrated resort of artists and centre of an important pilchard fishing industry, c. 1 mile S. of Penzance.

There is an art gallery where pictures painted locally are exhibited.

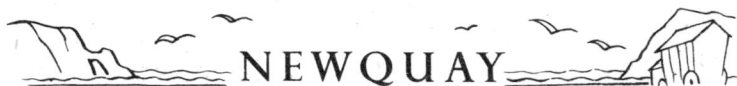

NEWQUAY

ONE of the most popular resorts in Cornwall, on the north coast, providing ample hotel and boarding-house accommodation, good sea-bathing on its wide sands (Fistral Bay, Towan, Bothwicks and Tolcarne beaches) liberally equipped with bathing cabins and tents.

There are tennis courts, bowling greens, an excellent 18-hole golf course (Newquay Golf Club), some trout fishing and good sea-fishing and boating. There are three cinemas and two theatres.

Padstow : St. George's Well.

PADSTOW. A small town and seaport, golfing and fishing centre on the estuary of the Camel near the north coast.

There is an 18-hole golf course near Trevose Head, and another, St. Enodoc, also with 18 holes, on the north bank of the Camel. Bathing is available near the Doom Bar, an immense sandbank lower down the estuary. There are trout to be caught in the river near the town. Padstow has a cinema and a concert hall.

On May day a festival called 'the Hobby Horse' is celebrated here. The ancient church is dedicated to St. Petrock.

Prideaux Place, on the site of an ancient monastery, was built by the Prideaux family in the sixteenth century and has extensive grounds.

Excursions to Trevose Head, Constantine Church and Harlyn Bay should be made from Padstow.

PAR. A small seaport on the south coast, c. 9 miles S. of Bodmin. There are bowling greens and a cinema here.

PENRYN. An ancient borough and market town on Penryn River, a branch of Falmouth Harbour, c. 2 miles NW. of Falmouth.

There are some remains here of Glassiney Collegiate Church, a thirteenth-century foundation.

PENZANCE

A BOROUGH and seaport, the most westerly town in England, on the south coast overlooking Mounts Bay. This is an excellent centre for sea-fishing, boating, bathing, golf (West Cornwall Golf Club at Lelant, 6 miles to the north-east), tennis and bowling. It has hotels, boarding-houses and attractive shops in great profusion, as well as a free library, an important subscription library, open-air bathing pool, cinemas and concert halls. The principal shops are in Market Jew Street, and close by are the Guildhall and Municipal Offices.

Sub-tropical plants grow in the beautiful Morrab gardens and other open spaces include Penrose and St. Anthony's gardens. There is an attractive sea-front and promenade. Penzance has four cinemas.

REDRUTH. A market and mining town, c. 9 miles W. of Truro.

It has bowling greens and two cinemas.

SALTASH. A borough overlooking the estuary of the Tamar, here crossed by the immense Royal Albert Bridge, c. 19 miles SSE. of Launceston.

There is good sea fishing to be had near the town, which also offers bowling greens and a cinema.

SILVERTON. A former market town, c. 8 miles NNE. of Exeter.

Tregonbus : on the road from Penzance to Land's End.

SCILLY ISLES

THESE isles lie 30 miles to the west of Land's End. Five of the islands—St. Mary's, Tresco, St. Martin's, St. Agnes and Bryher—are inhabited, there being some two hundred isles altogether in the archipelago.

The growing of flowers for the London market is the principal occupation of the inhabitants, but the islands are becoming increasingly popular with tourists for their excellent recreational facilities—boating, sea and sun-bathing, sea-fishing, golf, etc.

ST. MARY'S is the largest island, its capital being Hugh Town. There is a 9-hole golf course. Star Castle, commanding fine views of the islands, is Elizabethan in origin.

TRESCO is probably the most beautiful island. There are remains of an ancient abbey here and of Charles' Castle. Camphor, aloe and eucalyptus flourish here in the gardens of The Abbey mansion.

ST. AGNES is third in size; **ST. MARTINS** fourth; and **BRYHER** fifth.

FISHING IN CORNWALL

FALMOUTH. This is an excellent spot for pollack, but the 'marks' must be known. Mackerel are often to be caught in large numbers.

FOWEY. Mackerel, pollack, and whiting—the last-mentioned sometimes in great quantities—are to be taken off Fowey. Gurnards and bream are also caught. Fresh pilchard and mussel are the usual baits.

HELFORD. The coastal waters here provide conger fishing and pollack, mackerel, mullet, soles, plaice and bass.

LOOE. All along the coast in the neighbourhood of Looe whiting, pollack, mackerel, and dabs are to be caught in greater or lesser quantities.

MEVAGISSEY. Good pollack fishing is available here. Mussels may be obtained locally for bait.

POLPERRO. The fishing here is excellent and similar in character to that obtainable at Looe.

Trout Streams

CAMEL. A good stream offering small trout in large numbers, rising near Boscastle and flowing with a tortuous course to the sea at Padstow Bay.
Flies (brown trout):
Red Palmer.
Blue Dun.
Cochybonddhu.

FOWEY. A river rising near Brown Willy and flowing to the south coast past Liskeard and Lostwithiel.
Flies (brown trout):
March Brown.
Red Palmer.
Black Palmer.
In addition to the above the Lynher, Innery, Ottery, Hel and Fal provide trout fishing.

STRATTON. A pleasantly situated market town, c. 18 miles NNW. of Launceston. Its fine church has an interesting tower, roof and bench ends, as well as some mediæval glass.

The site of the battle of Stamford Hill, where Cornishmen defeated Parliamentarian forces in 1643 during the Civil Wars, lies near the town.

TORPOINT. A small town on the west bank of the Hamoaze, c. 3 miles W. of Plymouth. There is a golf course here.

TRURO

A CITY and excellent holiday centre, on the Kenwyn and Allen, two small streams which unite here to form the Truro river.

The Cathedral, designed by J. L. Pearson, R.A. in the Early English style, is constructed of Cornish materials and was begun in 1880. It is 300 feet long and 158 feet across the transepts; the centre tower and spire being 250 and the western towers 204 feet high. A wooden pulpit,

On Stamford Hill : Stratton.

some good ancient glass and a waggon roof were taken from the older church of St. Mary on this site, portions of which were incorporated in the building. Particular attention should be given to the excellent modern reredos.

The principal shops and hotels of Truro are in Boscawen Street.

The Museum of the Royal Institution of Cornwall contains good natural history and prehistoric collections, as well as a valuable library and art gallery.

Ancient buildings include what was formerly Truro Grammar School in St. Mary's Street, and open spaces are Waterfall and Victoria Gardens on the Kenwyn stream. Boscawen Park to the south of the city contains flower gardens and lakes, as well as tennis courts.

Truro has tennis courts, bowling greens and three cinemas.

WADEBRIDGE. A market town on the Camel, here spanned by an ancient bridge of fifteen arches built in 1485, c. 8 miles WNW. of Bodmin. To the S. the scenery is exceptionally fine. There is trout fishing in the Camel and sea-fishing at Padstow. Fine ancient churches may be visited at St. Breock and Egloshayle to the S.

St. Enodoc Golf Course (18 holes) is within easy access.

Wadebridge has tennis courts, bowling greens and a cinema.

Rocks on the Cornish Coast

Mullion Cove.

Cornish Villages
and
Beauty Spots

ALTARNUN, c. 8 miles WSW. of Launceston. Its church has a fine Perpendicular tower, good bench-ends and rood screen.

There was formerly a famous holy well here, the waters of which were reputed to cure madness.

ST. ANTHONY – IN – MEN-EAGE, c. 6 miles S. of Falmouth, has an ancient church said to have been founded by shipwrecked Normans.

ANTONY, c. 20 miles SSE. of Launceston. There are monuments in the church to the Pole-Carew family, whose seat is at East Antony near by.

BOCONNOC, c. 20 miles SW. of Launceston. Boconnoc mansion, formerly belonging to the Pitt family, stands in extensive wooded grounds. The first William Pitt was born here. There is an interesting ancient church.

ST. BREAGE, a village c. 12 miles WSW. of Falmouth, with interesting mediæval wall paintings in its church.

ST. BREOCK. See WADEBRIDGE.

BROWN WILLY, the highest peak in Cornwall (1,380 feet), 12 miles WSW. of Launceston.

ST. BURYAN, c. 5 miles SW. of Penzance. Its ancient Perpendicular church has a fine western tower.

CAPE CORNWALL, c. 4 miles N. of Land's End, has vestiges of an ancient chapel.

CARBIS BAY. See ST. IVES.

CARLYON BAY. See CHARLES-TOWN.

CASTLE–AN–DINAS. See ST. COLUMB MAJOR.

CHEEZEWRING. See ST. CLEER.

ST. CLEER, c. 12 miles E. of Bodmin, has remains of a former ancient well chapel with a holy well. The church has a good tower.

One mile to the NE. lie Trevethy Stones, an imposing cromlech consisting of six upright stones and one huge table slab. The Cheezewring, a remarkable stone pile, lies some 3 to 4 miles N. of the Trevethy Stones.

ST. CLETHER, on the Inney, here affording good trout fishing, c. 9 miles W. of Launceston, has an ancient holy well and well chapel.

CONSTANTINE, on the Helford, c. 5 miles SW. of Falmouth. There are notable oyster fisheries here. Constantine church is an ancient granite structure.

CRAFTHOLE, c. 7 miles W. of Plymouth, has an excellent 18-hole golf course (Whitsand Bay Golf Club).

CRANTOCK, or **ST. CRAN-TOCK,** a peaceful village to the W. of Newquay.

DOZMARY POOL. See BODMIN.

DULOE, c. 14 miles ESE. of Bodmin. There is an ancient church and a holy well here, both dedicated to St. Cuby, and, close by, a well-known stone circle.

ST. ENODOC. See PADSTOW.

EGLOSKERRY, c. 4 miles WNW. of Launceston. Near it is the ancient Penheale Manor. The church in Egloskerry is mainly Norman in style.

ENDELLION, or **ST. ENDEL-LION,** a village c. 10 miles NW. of Bodmin.

FAL, a river rising in central Cornwall, flowing through Grampound to Falmouth Harbour.

FLUSHING, a small village to the

N. of Falmouth, founded by Dutch settlers. It has an oyster fishery.

FORRABURY. *See* BOSCASTLE.

GERMOE, or **ST. GERMOE,** *c.* 9 miles E. of Penzance, has a quaint little church.

GODOLPHIN, overlooked by Godolphin Hill, *c.* 11 miles NNE. of Penzance. Godolphin Hall here, former seat of the family of that name, is now a farm house.

GOONBELL, a village to the SE. of St. Agnes.

GORRAN HAVEN, a fishing hamlet, *c.* 17 miles SSW. of Bodmin.

GULVAL, *c.* 2 miles NNE. of Penzance The ancient church contains monuments to its benefactors, the Bolitho family.

GUNWALLOE, or **WINWAL-LOE,** on the south coast, *c.* 12 miles SW. of Falmouth, has an old church with a detached tower.

GURNARD'S HEAD, a fine headland on the north coast, *c.* 7 miles NNW. of Penzance.

GWENNAP, *c.* 7 miles SW. of Truro, former centre of a rich mining district. In the Gwennap Pit here Wesley preached outstandingly to large congregations.

GWINEAR, *c.* 10 miles NW. of Penzance, has a church in the Perpendicular style with rich oak carving and a notable western tower. In its churchyard is an ancient cross.

GWITHIAN, overlooks St. Ives Bay, *c.* 12 miles NW. of Penzance. St. Gothian's Oratory, discovered in the sand here, is among the oldest churches surviving, dating probably from the eighth century.

HARLYN BAY, *c.* 2 miles W. of Padstow, scene of the discovery, in 1900, of a remarkable neolithic cemetery.

HINGSTON DOWN. *See* CAL-LINGTON.

ST. IVE (eev), a village *c.* 11 miles S. of Launceston, with an ancient church.

INDIAN QUEENS, a hamlet to the S. of St. Columb Major.

ST. JUST–IN–ROSELAND, on Carrick Roads, *c.* 9 miles SSE. of Truro, has an interesting old church close to the water's edge.

ST. KEVERNE, near the south coast, *c.* 9 miles S. of Falmouth. It has an old church with a conspicuous tower and spire.

Off the coast here are the ill-famed Manacle Rocks.

ST. KEW, *c.* 10 miles ENE of Padstow. The fifteenth-century church contains some remarkable ancient glass of the same date, mostly brought hither from Bodmin.

ST. KEYNE, *c.* 14 miles ESE. of Bodmin. About ½ mile to the E. is the famous holy well of St. Keyne.

KILKHAMPTON, *c.* 23 miles NNW. of Launceston, has associations with the famous Grenville family, especially in its fine old church.

KYNANCE COVE, styled by many ' the finest cove in the kingdom,' lies to the NW. of Lizard Head, notable for its caves, cliffs, and rocky islets. Sea-bathing is to be had here.

LANDEWEDNACK, on the Lizard, *c.* 15 miles SSW. of Falmouth. It has an ancient church with several features of local serpentine stone.

LAND'S END, the most westerly point of England. Off the dangerous coast here are Longships and Wolf Lighthouses, and there is a large

Land's End

cavern known as Land's End Hole. From Land's End the Scilly Isles may be seen on a very clear day.

LANDULPH, *c.* 18 miles SE. of Launceston. There is an inscription on brass in its fifteenth-century church to Theodore Palæologus of Pesaro in Italy, a lineal descendant of the Christian emperors of Greece, who was buried here in 1636.

LANHYDROCK, *c.* 2 miles S. of Bodmin, contains Lanhydrock House, with a noble barbican dated 1651 and a fine sycamore avenue.

LANIVET, *c.* 3 miles SW. of Bodmin. St. Benet's Abbey, formerly a seat of the Courtenays, includes portions of an ancient monastery.

LANTEGLOS–BY–FOWEY, *c.* 11 miles SSE. of Bodmin, has an interesting ancient church.

LAUNCELLS, *c.* 15 miles NNW. of Launceston, has good bench ends and mediæval encaustic tiles in its Perpendicular church.

LELANT. *See* ST. IVES.

ST. LEVAN, near the coast, *c.* 8 miles SW. of Penzance, has an ancient little church.

LINKINHORNE, *c.* 9 miles S. of Launceston. The fine late Pointed church here has a tower 120 feet high.

LONGSHIPS LIGHTHOUSE. *See* LAND'S END.

MADRON or **ST, MADRON,** *c.* 2 miles NW. of Penzance. It has an interesting church (see the humorous epitaph to George Daniel in the church yard), and close by a wishing well and the remains of a baptistry.

Two miles N. is Lanyon Quoit, a cromlech.

MANACCAN, *c.* 7 miles SSW. of Falmouth, has a fine doorway in its ancient church.

MANACLE ROCKS. *See* ST. KEVERNE.

ST. MAWES, a fishing village and holiday resort, *c.* 3 miles from Falmouth by ferry. There is a holy well here. The castle dates from 1542, and protected the entrance to the harbour.

MAWGAN. 1. **MAWGAN–IN–PYDAR,** or **ST. MAWGAN,** *c* 14 miles W. of Bodmin, has a fine pinnacled tower on its Late Pointed Church.

2. **MAWGAN–IN–MENEAGE,** *c.* 8 miles SW. of Falmouth. Its church has also a pinnacled tower.

Some Fishing Baits & Methods

	Method	Bait
WHITING		fresh pilchard
COD		fresh mackerel
HADDOCK	ground line	mussel
DABS		lug-worm
GURNARDS etc.		fresh herring
POLLACK	1. Drift or tideway fishing	live sand-eels
		lampreys
		rag-worm
		live shrimp
	2. 'Whiffing'	dead eel
		dead lamprey
		artificial spinning
		worm or eel
MACKEREL	1. Twenty to thirty feet of line behind moving boat	mackerel tail
		dead sand-eel
		artificial lures
	2. Ground fishing in the autumn	fresh pilchard
		squid
		live sand-eel
BASS	1. Fly-fishing from a boat	any bright artificial lure
	2. Ground-fishing with leger	squid
		live sand-eel
		dead sand-eel
	3. Drift-line fishing	live sand-eel
	4. 'Whiffing'	dead sand-eel
		artificial eels
CONGER	Hand line, especially at dusk or in darkness	squid
		any fresh fish

ST. MICHAEL'S MOUNT. *See* MARAZION.

ST. MINVER HIGHLANDS, ST. MINVER LOWLANDS. Two villages some 4 miles to the NE. of Padstow. The former has an interesting old church, and the latter a holy well.

MORWENSTOW, in a deep valley near the north coast, c. 20 miles NNW. of Launceston. It has a fine church with Norman and possibly earlier features, and, on a precipice, a holy well dedicated to St. Morwen. Tonacombe Manor, of thirteenth-century origin, is near at hand.

MOUSEHOLE, c. 3 miles SW. of Penzance. This place was destroyed by Spaniards in 1597. It was the birthplace of Dolly Pentreath, allegedly the last to speak Cornish. Off the coast here are St. Clement's Islands.

MULLION, near the south coast, c. 12 miles SW. of Falmouth. Near it is the picturesque Mullion Cove, a pilchard fishing centre, with a small harbour, and Mullion Island. There is an 18-hole golf course at Mullion.

ST. NEOT, c. 8 miles E. of Bodmin. Its church (1321) has some excellent fifteenth-century stained glass windows recording the life of St. Neot, said to have been a relative of King Alfred.

PAUL, c. 3 miles SW. of Penzance, has an ancient church with a fine tower, and in the yard the grave of Dolly Pentreath, last speaker of the Cornish tongue.

PELYNT, c. 13 miles SE. of Bodmin. There is an ancient holy well dedicated to St. Nonna here. Trelawne, to the SE. of Pelynt, was formerly the seat of the Trelawneys, and dates in part from the fifteenth century.

There are numerous prehistoric remains near the village.

PENTEWAN, a small port on the south coast, c. 4 miles S. of St. Austell, with good bathing and sea-fishing facilities.

PERRANARWORTHAL, a village, c. 6 miles NNW. of Falmouth.

PERRANPORTH, a popular resort, c. 9 miles NW. of Truro, with magnificent sandy beaches and cliff scenery. There is excellent sea-bathing, an 18-hole golf course, tennis courts, and a cinema.

PERRANUTHNOE, c. 6 miles E. of Penzance, a popular bathing and picnicing place. It has an ancient church with a Perpendicular tower.

PERRANZABULOE, or ST. PIRAN-IN-THE-SANDS, c. 7 miles NW. of Truro, is famous for the oratory of St. Piran, near Perran Bay, some 3 miles to the N., possibly a sixth or seventh-century building buried for many hundred years in the sands here.
St. Piran's Round, an ancient amphi-theatre, lies about 2 miles N. of Perranzabuloe.

POLPERRO, a quaint fishing village and picturesque resort, built in a gorge on the south coast, c. 15 miles SE. of Bodmin. Polperro was formerly notorious as a retreat of smugglers, and is now much frequented by painters.

POLRUAN. *See* FOWEY.

PORTH CURNOW, on the south coast, c. 9 miles SW. of Penzance. There are fragmentary remains here of one of the most ancient chapels in Cornwall. An open-air theatre was opened here in 1935.

PORTHLEVEN, a fishing port and a tourist resort of increasing importance, on the south coast, c. 3 miles SW. of Helston.

A Village Street in the South-West.

PORT ISAAC, a bathing, tennis, fishing, and walking resort on Port Isaac Bay, on the north coast, *c.* 10 miles NW. of Bodmin. The harvest festival at Port Isaac church is interesting, where fishing paraphernalia takes the place of the usual flower and fruit offerings.

POUGHILL (puf-il), *c.* 20 miles NNW. of Launceston. Its ancient church has a fine Perpendicular tower, carved bench ends and large mediæval wall paintings of St. Christopher.

PRAA SANDS. *See* MARAZION.

PROBUS, *c.* 5 miles NNE. of Truro. The magnificent ornamented tower on its church is over 100 feet in height. Parts of the chancel screen date from the sixteenth century.

PRUSSIA COVE. *See* MARAZION.

RAME HEAD, the headland which commands Plymouth Sound on the west. On it is the village of Rame, with an early church.

RESTORMEL. *See* LOSTWITHIEL.

ROCHE, *c.* 8 miles SW. of Bodmin. The high Roche Rocks here are surmounted by the remains of an ancient chapel and a hermit's cave. There is a holy well close by. Roche church has an ornate Norman font.

SANCREED, *c.* 4 miles W. of Penzance, has a fine fifteenth-century church. Near by is a well-known prehistoric stone circle called Boscawen-Un.

SENNEN, a fishing port, *c.* 9 miles WSW. of Penzance, reputedly scene in ancient days of a great victory by King Arthur over the Danes. A large monolith near Sennen Church commemorates the event. Sea-angling is at its best here, and there is bathing at Sennen Cove, a village on Whitesand Bay to the NW. Pilchards, mullet, crabs, and lobsters are caught in great profusion at Sennen.

Land's End is about 1 mile to the SW.

SHEVIOCK, *c.* 7 miles W. of Plymouth. The ancient church is Decorated and Perpendicular in style. There is an 18-hole golf course (Whitsand Bay Club) at Portwrinkle on Whitesand Bay to the S.

SUMMERCOURT, a hamlet *c.* 5 miles S. of St. Columb Major.

TINTAGEL, a village, properly known as Trevena, and a headland on the north coast, *c.* 15 miles N. of Bodmin. There is an 18-hole golf course here. Tintagel Head, a great peninsular cliff known as 'the island,' surmounted by the remains of Tintagel Castle, lies to the W. The Castle was allegedly the birthplace of King Arthur, and remains of a Celtic monastery have been discovered in the excavations here. It was an early residence of the earls of Cornwall, as also was part of the ancient church on the cliffs to the S.

There is sea-bathing at Bossiney Cove, *c.* 1 mile N. of the village.

TREVETHY STONES. *See* St. Cleer.

TREVOSE HEAD, a headland with a lighthouse on the north coast, *c.* 4 miles W. of Padstow. There is an 18-hole golf course close by (Trevose Golf Club).

TYWARDREATH, a village near the south coast, *c.* 9 miles S. of Bodmin, anciently seat of a Benedictine priory.

WARBSTOW, *c.* 12 miles WNW. of Launceston, has, near it, an outstanding ancient British camp known as Warbstow Barrows.

WEEK ST. MARY, a village *c.* 12 miles NW. of Launceston. It has associations with Thomasine Bonaventure, a sixteenth-century native who, by three fortunate marriages, rose from herd girl to local benefactress.

WHITESAND BAY. *See* Sennen; Sheviock.

ST. WINNOW, on the Fowey, *c.* 8 miles SSE. of Bodmin, has some ancient stained glass in its Perpendicular church.

WOLF LIGHTHOUSE. *See* Land's End.

ZENNOR, on the north coast, *c.* 5 miles W. of St. Ives. In its ancient church is a carved bench end commemorating the alleged enticement by a mermaid of the local squire's son. The Giant's Rock lies near the church, and the famous Zennor Cromlech should also be visited. There are numerous other remains of antiquity in the neighbourhood.

Quaker Meeting House near Falmouth.

The Scilly Islands

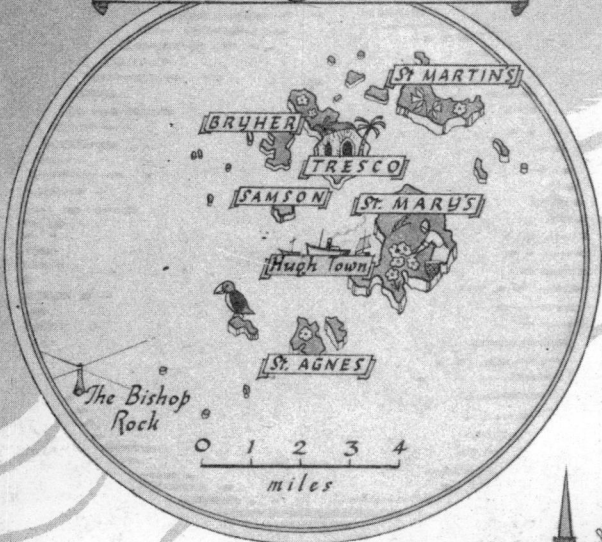

St Martins

BRUHER

TRESCO

SAMSON

St MARYS

Hugh Town

St AGNES

The Bishop Rock

0 1 2 3 4
miles

NEWQU

Holy Well

Subme
City

Perranporth

St AGNES

TRUR

St IVES

The Cutty Sark

The Furry Dance

FALMOUTH

Pixie Hall

PENZANCE

MARAZION

HELSTON

NEWLYN

Logan Rock

Land's End

St MICHAELS MOUNT

ance to Scilly 36 mls. Islands

Lizard Poi